Bought in December 2001 from Dennis Tri-angle Publishing.

Never met Bert Holland, but this is c excellent book, along with `Lancashire Tri-angle` 1 +2.

Most of the locations are ~~noto~~ now unregonisable as most of the cuttings are filled in, and built over. Station sites, goods yards. It takes a lot of local Knowledge. especially in the Bolton area to get now and then shots.

Of Particular interest is the map on page 37 of Lever St Yard, I used to live at 349 the house on the corner, and my first interest of railways was watching the trains shunting in the sidings, an excellent view from the upstairs back bedroom window!

From memory I remember a W.D. 2-8-0 lying on its side just the other side of Clarendon St Bridge circa 1960, also remember seeing Jubilee 45552 "Silver Jubilee" on the Manchester line about the same time.

If events had taken another course, Great moor St. Station would still be open today, alas re-sited in Crook St. Yard Modern D.M.U. Trains would be running to manchester via Plodder Lane, Little Hulton, and Walkden providing a fast service and taking some of the overloading problems off the Trinity Street Route, and also relieving traffic, congestion! If only people had listned in the 1950's.

PLODDER LANE FOR

FARNWORTH

BY

BERT HOLLAND

TRIANGLE

PUBLISHING

Copyright © Bert Holland.
First Published 2001 by Triangle Publishing.
British Library Cataloguing in Publication Data.
Holland H.L.
Plodder Lane For Farnworth.
ISBN 0 9529 333 6 5
Printed in England by :
The Amadeus Press Ltd, Bradford.
Text by Bert Holland.
Edited and compiled for publication by
D.J.Sweeney.
Maps by Bert Holland.
Cover design by Scene, Print & Design Ltd,
Leigh, Lancs.
Designed and published by
Triangle Publishing,
509, Wigan Road,
Leigh, Lancs. WN7 5HN.
Tel: 01942/677919
www.trianglepublishing.co.uk

Front Cover. B.R.Standard class 5 No.73033 is seen in Crook Street yard prior to departing with the daily freight for Patricroft on 17th August 1965. Behind the engine is Fletcher Street bridge, underneath which, diverging to the right is the steeply graded original formation of the Bolton & Leigh Railway of 1828, now the branch to High Street and Magee's Sidings, with the double track formation of 1875 to Roe Green and Atherton on the left. In the fork of the junction is Bolton No.2 signal box, usually referred to as Fletcher Street.

Photo, Author.

Plate 1. The junction in Bolton of the lines to Plodder Lane and Atherton was in a dark, fenced-in cutting, difficult to photograph from any location other than the trackside, so photographs of it are rare. This undated but late period view shows Class 8F 2-8-0 No.48536 heading tender first for the Plodder Lane direction, with the lines to Atherton on the right.

Photo, Bolton Museums and Art Gallery.

Plate 2.. Stanier Class 5 No.45495, working hard on the 1 in 60 incline between Bolton and Daubhill with the third excursion train of the day from Great Moor St. to North Wales, seen passing Townson's 'Cygnet' joinery works on 26th. June 1954. The photograph is taken from Ellesmere Road.   Photo, C.B.Golding.

Rear Cover, main picture. Taken from the brakevan of a train that by this time was the only remnant of the once intense goods and mineral service worked by Plodder Lane engines and men. On 17th. August 1965, BR class 5 4-6-0 73033 of Patricroft sheds waits by the water tank at Crook St. yard, Bolton, prior to working the daily freight to Patricroft. Fletcher Street bridge is visible beyond the engine, and to the right are the remains of the disused cattle dock. The maroon and cream shunter's cabin is clearly visible on the near side of the bridge, and to its right, behind the cattle dock, is the brick-built shunter's and yard facilities block constructed in the late 1950's to replace a collection of grounded carriage bodies. The train would stop en route to shunt at Daubhill and Atherton before joining the Wigan-Tyldesley direct line at Howe Bridge East Junction.

Rear cover (top) 73033 is seen broadside in Crook St. yard on the same day shunting. Overlooking the scene is the Bolton Corporation bus depot the vehicles of which are also history.

Rear cover (bottom). Class 3F 0-6-0T, No. 47378 shunting the Dawes St. coal drops alongside Bolton Gt. Moor St. station in the late winter snow of 16th. March 1964. The locomotive is carrying on its smokebox a board with the number 62, perhaps the trip number of its duty from Patricroft shed. The number of wagons in the train is impressive for this late date. The remains of the passenger station are located behind the wagon parked in the siding on the left.

Photos, Author.

3

CONTENTS

Plate 3. The goods shed at Plodder Lane, as viewed from the approach road that led into the goods yard from the corner of Plodder Lane and Bradford Road. The goods yard had two sidings from each of the north and south ends, and all four sets of buffer stops can be seen here. Also visible in the right background is the yard crane. The date is 21st. July. 1964.   Photo, Author.

ACKNOWLEDGEMENTS

This book is unusual in more than one respect: it was conceived in Bolton in 1963, most the data was collected during the 1990's while I was in Canada, and the writing was done during a four month period that I spent in Austria in early 2000. The story of Plodder Lane has therefore been a long time in the making, and during this process has travelled further from Plodder Lane than most of the coal or passengers carried on the trains that it describes.

The story began with an enquiry that I placed in the Railway Modeller of March 1963, the first letter that I received on the subject, from Mr. K. Smith of Appleton, Nr. Warrington, being dated February 24th. of that year. Over the intervening years other interests came and went, I moved from school to university and then to a position in Canada, but Plodder Lane was always there, if only in the distant background. In the middle 90's, however, after 30 years of collecting data, it was time to act!

By this time many people had been involved in providing information, but several stand out or special mention. Brian Wesley, now in London, with whom in 1963 I first walked the line from Bolton Great Moor St. to Plodder Lane (including the dark, damp and smelly tunnel under the recreation grounds to Lever St.), has been involved from the start and his help with working timetables from the L&NWR and later periods has been invaluable. Richard Ball, living in Edinburgh, whose researches during trips to Bolton finally sorted out the web of details surrounding the private sidings and yards in the Crook St. area, and who was the source of a constant flow of maps and e-mails across the Atlantic Ocean, read the entire manuscript and kept me straight on a number of points. Brian, Richard, and I were all pupils at Canon Slade School in Bolton at a time when one of the teachers there was John Marshall. It was the latter who, by example, diverted our youthful interests from train spotting to other more serious aspects of railways, so he must take some credit for this book, in addition to supplying several of its photographs, and in many respects could be regarded as its 'grandfather'.

A special acknowledgement is due to Jim Jones of Farnworth. When he first contacted me in 1993 it was apparent from both the quality and quantity of his recollections of Plodder Lane shed that the time had come to put 'Plodder Lane' down on paper. Jim started a 43 year railway footplate career at Plodder Lane in March 1941, transferring to Burnden sheds in March 1946, and either directly or through his contacts with former enginemen provided almost all the material for Chapter 5 in a series of long letters written over an 8 year period, during which we met on several occasions during my trips to the UK.

Many others have been helpful in providing recollections, information, and photographs over the years. In all these categories both Harry Jack, who lived in Plodder Lane in the 1940's, and Cyril Golding, who lived and photographed in the Bolton area in the 1950's, have been invaluable resources. Other individuals who have contributed to this work are Colin Brooks (Bolton), Alan Crompton (Weston, Ontario), Ken Fairey (Wellingborough), Gregory Fox (Stockport), Graham Hardy (Dewsbury), Bob Hayes (Swinton), Geoff Hayes (Auchtermuchty, Fife), J.C. Hillmer (Wilmslow), Brian Hilton (Shaw), M. Hogg (Bolton), Arthur Holland (Bolton), Ian Holt (Rochdale), Frank Hope (Yarm), Bernard Matthews (Sutton), Maureen and Alan Mitchell (Harwood), Steve McCombie (London), Herbert Morton (Stevenage), P.G. Pope (London), Harvey Scowcroft (Bolton), K. Smith (Appleton), Allan Sommerfield (Astley Bridge), Jim Tonge (Chipping Sodbury), and Stephen Wolstenholme (Purley). Thanks go to them, and also to the staffs of the Greater Manchester Record Office, the Farnworth Library, the Bolton Library Local History Section, the Bolton Museum, the Bolton Evening News, and the National Railway Museum, York. My gratitude is due to all those mentioned above, for without their help this story could not have been told.

Finally, thanks to Dennis Sweeney of Triangle Publishing, for his willingness to leave this subject to me, and his patience in waiting for the outcome. I hope the delay is justified by the result, but I leave that judgement to the reader.

A WORD OF EXPLANATION

Anyone describing a railway built in part almost two centuries ago, only 7 years after the death of Napoleon, and which ceased to exist almost forty years ago, has some choices to make. I have chosen to use the 24 hr. clock for reasons of simplicity and familiarity to the modern reader, except for those cases where times have been reproduced from original documents (e.g. the shunting and trip workings document used in the preparation of Chapter 4) where the flavour of the original would have been lost in translation. Currency has also been reported in its original units, with contemporary comparisons, and the same applies to the designation of areas.

Spelling is always a thorny issue, the present complications and their resolution being:

(a) Although the signal box (at least in BR days) carried the name Hulton Sidings, the L&NWR working timetables refer to Hulton Siding and the LM&SR and BR timetables use the name Hulton's Siding. A more accurate description would have been Hulton's Sidings, but this versions seems never to have found official favour. I have opted for Hulton Sidings as it was the name on the box in latter years and, in my view, represents the best compromise of the three.

(b) Plodder Lane, known for some years by the L&NWR and LM&SR as Plodder Lane for Farnworth, is referred to for convenience by the shorter title.

(c) Although the ground frame itself and the L&NWR private sidings book used the name Highfield Siding, the yard appears in all the later working timetables as Highfield Sidings, and the latter version has been used throughout.

(d) Sanderson's Siding(s) is singular in official L&NWR documents, but became plural by LM&SR days only to revert to singular status in the BR working timetables. The singular version is used throughout

(e) Walkden Siding is singular in L&NWR days only, becoming Walkden Sidings under LM&SR and BR administrations. The later version appeared on the signal box and is the one used here.

(f) both spellings of 'break' and 'brake' have been used as they appear in contemporary documents.

(g) The abbreviation Jn. has been used for Junction. The L&NWR favoured Jc., the LM&SR used both, but BR standardised on Jn. in its working timetables.

Further information

Any endeavour of this kind tends to accumulate more information than can be conveniently presented in a single volume. For those interested in further information on the subject of Plodder Lane and its railways much of this extra material, including some photographs that have not been used in this book, is available on the internet at www.members.home.net/fholland5/index.html This web page will be updated from time to time as more information becomes available. The e-mail address for those who would like to contact me to discuss Plodder Lane, railways in general, the MGB, or any other subject you care to choose, is holland@chemiris.labs.brocku.ca.

INTRODUCTION

When the London and North Western Railway reached Plodder Lane in the Borough of Farnworth in 1874 it served a relatively isolated community of sixty nine houses and a church, built along a ridge of high land two miles to the south of Bolton town centre, and one mile west of Farnworth. Communication with Bolton was along country roads, passing by Wilken Hall, through meadows and copses of trees; to reach Farnworth, one could follow the lanes by Highfield Hall. Bolton had, however, taken advantage of this elevated location south of the town when, in 1861, the Union Workhouse was built on a 26.75 acre site just north of Plodder Lane, a site which came to include the Fever Isolation Hospital, the Hollin's Cottage Homes orphanage and school, and a mortuary chapel and burial ground.

The coming of the railway was to change the Plodder Lane community forever. A station was built south of the road, providing direct transport to both Bolton and Manchester, and a goods yard and engine shed were laid out north of Plodder Lane, the latter on land adjacent to the workhouse. A new Methodist Chapel, close to the engine sheds, was opened in 1888 and by the turn of the century the Plodder Lane community had expanded dramatically: the engine shed employed almost 200 men and provided a home for approximately 30 locomotives that worked trains over a large area of south western Lancashire.

For a period of sixty years from the coming of the rails until the mid-1930's little was to change for the railway: coal was shifted from the local pits, empty wagons returned there, and people were taken to Bolton, Manchester, and further afield. There was gradual change outside the world of the railway, however. The urban development of Bolton and Farnworth had progressed to encompass Plodder Lane. The once distinct community gradually disappeared into a larger urban melting pot, and the associated expansion of public road transport, together the decline of the coal industry, heralded a period of prolonged decay for the railway. Passenger trains ceased to run in 1954, the engine sheds closed in the same year, and goods services lasting only a little longer, until 1965. Gradually the railway land reverted to others uses. The site of the engine shed became a housing development, the railway station site vanished under landfill, and now there is little evidence of the railway activity that once centred on Plodder Lane. This account of the development and operation of the railway in the Plodder Lane area recalls the time when engines left the shed to take goods trains to Leeds or Liverpool, haul coal away from the Bridgewater Collieries pits, or transport office workers from Bolton and the local stations to Manchester on a railway that is no more than a memory.

Bert Holland,
Ontario, 2001.

Chapter 1.

The London & North Western Railway in Bolton

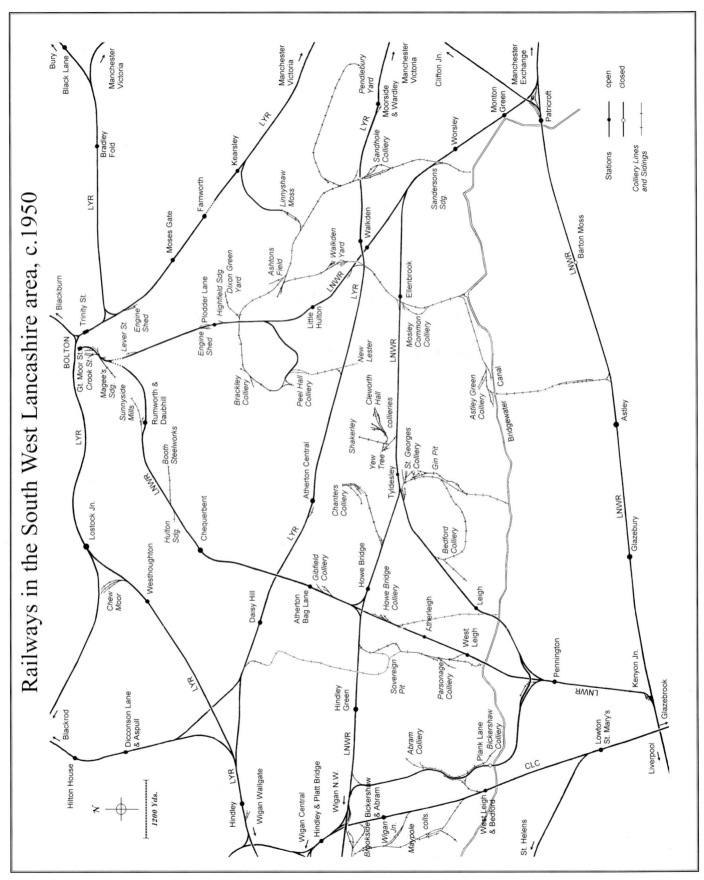

Railways in the South West Lancashire area, c.1950

10

EARLY DEVELOPMENTS OF THE RAILWAYS OF BOLTON

The London and North Western Railway Company had a presence in Bolton long before the construction of any facilities at Plodder Lane took place in the 1870's. It is not the intention of this volume to cover the early history of the L&NWR and its predecessor companies in the Bolton area in any detail, as this information can be found in a number of books listed in the bibliography. Nevertheless, an understanding of the early history of the railway that linked the Bolton Crook Street and Great Moor Street areas with the outside world is useful in understanding the developments that occurred in the 1870's and later, and for this reason a brief outline of the developments that produced the railway as it existed prior to the expansions that began in 1870 will be presented.

The Bolton and Leigh Railway, engineered by George Stephenson and opened throughout in March 1830, was the first in Lancashire and one of the earliest railways in the British Isles, pre-dating the better known Liverpool and Manchester Railway by six months: a section of the B&L line between Pendlebury Fold and the Lecturer's Closes in Bolton had actually been operating since August 1828. The completed Bolton & Leigh Railway placed the former town in the forefront of railway development in the British Isles, assisting an already established cotton industry in the movement of raw and finished goods. Perhaps of greater importance, the railway allowed the mills of Bolton direct access to the rich coals seams of the Leigh area, and also to those of the Wigan area via connections with the established canal network .

The first railway terminus in Bolton was in an area known as the Lecturer's Closes, subsequently to be developed as the Crook Street goods yard, but within a short time a new terminus of the 7³/₄ mile line was built at street level to the south of Great Moor Street, adjacent to the Lecturer's Closes area. The route from Bolton to Leigh (and later, via the Kenyon and Leigh Junction Railway to the Liverpool and Manchester Railway at Kenyon Junction and thence to the railway network of the times) was not an easy one, but was typical of many railways of that period, for which rope haulage was the acceptable solution for dealing with any appreciable gradient. The summit of the line at Daubhill was reached from Bolton by rope haulage of the trains up a 62 chain (1.25 km) gradient shown on the original plans at 1 in 32.6, easing to 1 in 55 near the top. At Daubhill, locomotive haulage was used as far as Chequerbent, where a second stationary engine was used for the longer inclined plane of 1 mile 20 chains (2 km), laid out at 1 in 30 to 1 in 50, down to Atherton. It was the realignment of this latter incline that was notorious in later years for being susceptible to mining subsidence, resulting in a short section reputed to be as steep as 1 in 18.

The early lines in this area were built primarily to move coal from Hulton's collieries at Pendlebury Fold and Fletcher's collieries in Atherton, minerals and raw materials for the steel industry, and other raw and finished goods of various kinds. The cotton industry was dominant in the latter field, but the iron and steel industry, together with heavy engineering products, were also important contributors to railway income. Benjamin Hick of Hick and Rothwell, suppliers of early railway locomotives, was a prominent promoter of the Bolton and Leigh Railway and was also involved in the Union Foundry located north of Crook St. alongside Moor Lane, and served by a branch from the railway installations at Crook Street. Later known as the Bolton Iron and Steel Company, this foundry and the nearby goods warehouse on Deansgate continued to be served by rail until their closures in 1924 and 1930, respectively. In the meantime, Hick had established a large engineering works known as the Soho foundry on the south side of Crook St. in 1833, on a site later to become the home of Hick, Hargreaves & Co., near to which the Atlas Forge of Thomas Walmsley was opened in 1869.

The Bolton and Leigh Railway, together with the Kenyon and Leigh Junction Railway, was leased and run by John Hargreaves from 1831 until 1845. When the lease expired the line was taken over by the Grand Junction Railway, which in its turn was absorbed by the London & North Western Railway in 1846. The L&NWR thus established a position in Bolton that it would maintain until formation of the London Midland & Scottish Railway in 1923.

Plate 4. The staff of Gt. Moor St. station on platform 3 in 1921. Not counting the engine crew and the train's guard (on the right below the engine chimney), there are 23 people in this view, including the clerical staff (not wearing company uniforms), a sizeable compliment for a small station. The characteristic L&NWR 'non-slip' corrugated paving surface to the platforms is evident; this feature is visible in photographs to the end of the station's life.   Photo, Bolton Museums and Art Gallery.

EXPANSION

Although the Bolton Iron and Steel Co., the Soho Foundry, and Atlas Forge were to become closely associated with the railway through their extensive traffic and the use of private sidings, its was other factors that led the L&NWR to extend their facilities in Bolton by the construction of a direct line from Manchester in the early 1870's. Following the completion of their direct route from Manchester to Wigan via Tyldesley, Howe Bridge and Hindley Green in 1864, the L&NWR had direct access to many of the major collieries around Hindley and Tyldesley, but were still unable to access the potentially lucrative traffic from collieries north of these locations, particularly those of the Little Hulton area. Many of the pits in the latter area were to become linked in the 1870's by the Bridgewater Collieries railway system, centred on Walkden, and the possibility of tapping into this development must have been instrumental in the decision by the L&NWR to extend their Manchester-Wigan route northwards from Roe Green, between Worsley and Ellenbrook, towards the lucrative coal traffic

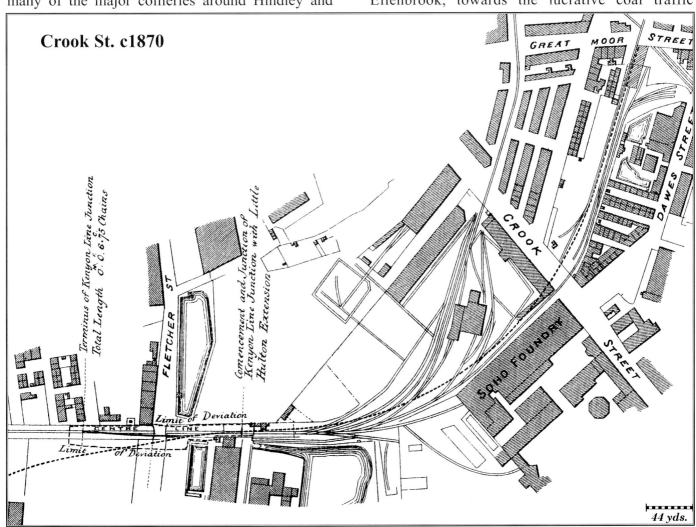

Crook St. c1870

This plan, taken from preliminary construction plans for the Little Hulton Extension Railway, shows the layout at Crook St. and Gt. Moor St. in Bolton as it was prior to construction of the direct line to Manchester. The latter is shown, bottom left, as a dotted line which makes connection with the single track Bolton and Leigh formation at the foot of the Daubhill incline, and then continues through Crook St. yard to the site of the new station at Gt. Moor St. The building in the centre of Crook St. yard with rail connections from both ends is thought to have been the original locomotive depot in Bolton.

13

hopefully to be generated at Walkden and Little Hulton.

A branch from Roe Green Junction to Little Hulton, together with connecting mineral lines to collieries in the local area, particularly at Walkden, was duly opened in 1870, but this was clearly regarded by the L&NWR as an interim measure, for by 1874 the connection with the Bolton and Leigh line at Fletcher Street in Bolton, known as the Little Hulton Extension Railway, had been made, allowing for the direct running of trains from Bolton to Manchester using this route, and the new facilities at Plodder Lane were well in hand.

Plate 5. The water column at the foot of the ramp leading to platform 4 at Bolton Gt. Moor St. This was of a standard L&NW design and still functional on 3rd December 1963. The curved cast iron plate on the column reads: "SV 12ft. to shut off water supply to carriage washing pipe."

Photo, Author.

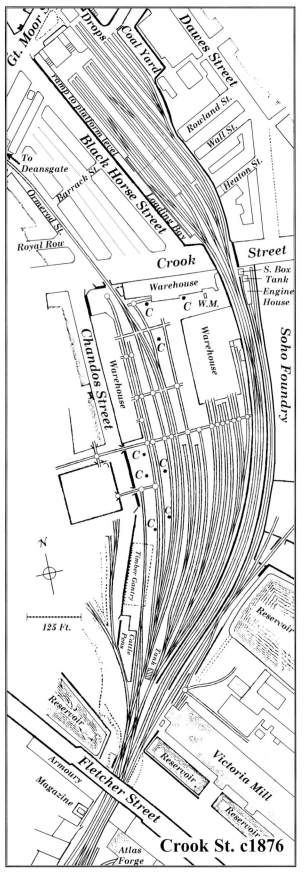

Crook St. c1876

Plate 6. A view of Crook St. goods yard on 7th December 1963, from the ramp to the passenger station. The new (1874) warehouse is prominent on the right, while the low buildings at the rear belong to the earlier warehouse, converted to stables and office accommodation when the yard facilities were expanded in the 1870's. The Chandos St. warehouse with canopies covering the wagons, used for fruit and vegetable traffic from the 1870's, is visible on the extreme left. Photo, Author.

Plate 7. The line to Atherton emerging from the tunnel underneath the recreation ground at Bolton. At the far end of the tunnel the line to Manchester joined this route at the junction south of Fletcher St. The date is 22nd July 1967.

Photo, J. Marshall.

The map of Crook St., opposite, is taken from the construction plans of the Little Hulton Extension Railway as updated in 1876 to illustrate the line as built, makes an interesting comparison with the plan of the area in 1870. The most prominent difference is the presence of the new passenger station at Gt. Moor St., together with the coal drops and coal yard on Dawes St. Crook St. yard has been considerably expanded, with a new warehouse adjoining the ramp to the passenger station, a timber gantry, cattle loading dock and water tank, but the original warehouses alongside Crook St. and Chandos St. are still present. The locomotive sheds in the Crook St. yard are now gone. Bolton No. 1 signal box is identified, as are the engine house and water tank for the hydraulic machinery now installed in the Crook St. yard. The line alongside the Soho Foundry running to the engine house is all that remains of the original route to the passenger station.

Plate 8. A view of the station approaches at the top of the ramp leading from Fletcher St. on 7th December 1963. The building to the left of the running lines is part of the Crook St. warehouse, and to right are, left to right, the Gt. Moor St. water tank, Bolton No. 1 signal box, the hydraulic accumulator tower for the machinery in the goods warehouse, and Hick, Hargreaves Soho Foundry. The down line and crossover were still in use at this time to serve the Dawes St. coal drops.   Photo, Author.

Plate 9. The Dawes St. coal drops as seen on 7th. December 1963. The original Hulton Colleries two-line 'coal viaduct' of 1874 was to the left of this more modern building. These sidings closed in 1936 and their terminus can be seen behind the bushes at the rear of the left hand wall. The newer building covers a site originally occupied by the three sidings of the Fletcher Burrows yard. As in many photographs taken in this area of Bolton, the town hall clock is a prominent feature.

Photo, Author.

16

THE LITTLE HULTON EXTENSION RAILWAY

The double track extension of the branch from Little Hulton to Fletcher St. Junction, Bolton, together with the 'Little Hulton Mineral Branch' from Little Hulton Junction to a number of collieries including the large Peel Hall Colliery complex of James Roscoe & Sons, was authorised by Act of Parliament on 12th. July 1869. Construction commenced at several points along the route in March 1871 and was complete by October 1874, with goods services commencing on November 16th. of that year. Completion of the facilities between Roe Green Jn. and Bolton to the standards necessary for passenger traffic was not carried out until 1st. April 1875, when a service from Bolton Great Moor Street to Manchester was inaugurated.

According to the official plan of the line, corrected in 1876 to reflect the facilities as built, the length of the line from Roe Green Junction to the new station at Great Moor Street in Bolton was 5 miles, 770 yards, giving a considerable reduction in the distance between Bolton and Manchester by L&NWR compared with this company's existing route via Chequerbent, Howe Bridge and Tyldesley, and an overall Bolton - Manchester (Exchange) distance of 12 miles, comparing favourably with the Lancashire and Yorkshire Railway's route of 10 miles in terms of distance but not, as will be seen, in terms of gradients. At the Bolton end the new line emerged from a 300 yard long tunnel to join the existing route from Atherton and Daubhill just south of Fletcher St. bridge, with the new Bolton No. 2 signal box located in the apex of the junction.

Plate 10. A view of the end of platforms 4 (extreme right) and 3 at Bolton Gt. Moor St. station, taken on 7th December 1963. The curved glass walled office accommodation at the end of platform 4 was a distinctive feature of the station. The smoke troughs over platforms 3 and 4 are still intact, that over platform 3 marking the spot where coal tanks would come to rest after working from Manchester.   Photo, Author.

Construction of this tunnel beneath the Heywood Recreation Ground was the subject of a complaint in the Bolton Evening News for 20th. October 1871, that local residents were in danger from falling rocks and earth thrown up by blasting, noting that one life had already been lost, an indication that the cut-and-cover method of construction was used and that the Health and Safety Regulations in 1871 left something to be desired.

The majority of the L&NWR trains to and from Bolton used Hunt's Bank (Victoria) station in Manchester, prior to completion of the L&NWR's new station at Manchester Exchange in 1884, when the train service from Bolton was concentrated on the latter station. However, until the first decade of the twentieth century several trains to and from Bolton, including the through carriages to London (Euston), used London Road station in Manchester via the connection from Ordsall Lane.

Crook St., c1930.

This plan shows the lines in the Crook St. area at their fullest extent. At the top, the former L&YR lines from Bolton Trinity St. to Lostock Junction can be seen, adjacent to which (but on a higher level), Gt. Moor St. station is shown with its overall roof at the full original length. The single line to the Deansgate warehouse is seen crossing Crook St. and running along Ormrod St. The signal gantry across the tracks leading to the passenger station is identified, as are both signal boxes. Bridgeman St. goods warehouse, formerly the Victoria Mill, with its south-western extension, is shown located in the angle of Fletcher St. and Bridgeman St. Compared with the 1876 layout, the yard has considerably expanded to the west of Chandos St. Atlas forge is located to the south of the junction between the single track Bolton and Leigh route and the double track of the Little Hulton Extension Line.

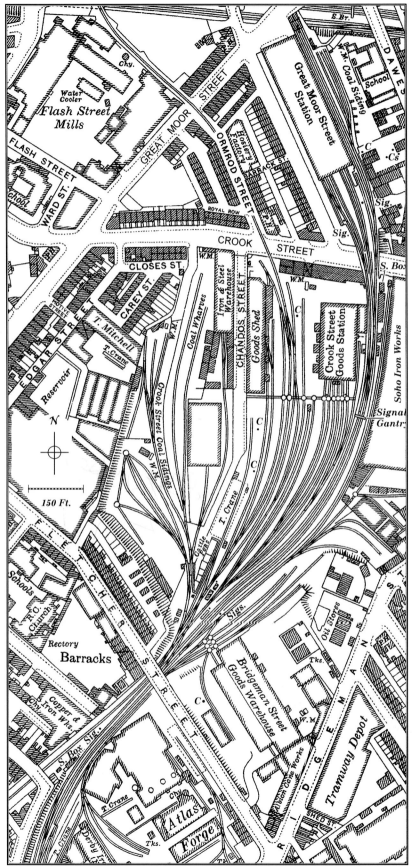

CHANGES IN BOLTON

Cable haulage on the incline to Daubhill and between Chequerbent and Atherton had ceased by the late 1850's, and the difficulties associated with the subsequent working of the line by locomotive power were to be a factor in the decision to upgrade the Bolton to Leigh section in the late 1870's. At this time, much of this route was still the original single track formation with its steep gradients, and this, together with an increase in traffic following the completion of the direct Manchester route, also caused operational difficulties. The runaway down the grade from Daubhill in 1858 of a loaded goods train in charge of 2-4-0 tank locomotive *Redstart*

caused considerable damage to the original Bolton and Leigh Railway passenger station at Great Moor Street in Bolton, and while the station was rebuilt and was presumably able to cope with traffic in the Leigh and Kenyon direction, it would clearly be inadequate for the additional traffic generated by the direct connection to Manchester. On 1st. August 1871 the old station, located at street level on Great Moor Street, was closed, and traffic handled in a temporary terminus in the Crook St. yard, probably using the warehouse alongside Chandos Street, until the new station at Great Moor St. was opened on 28th. September 1874. The new station was built in

*Plate 11.*The view southwards down the passenger ramp from Crook St. bridge on 7th. December 1963. The building on the left is part of the Hick, Hargreaves Soho Foundry and that on the right is part of the Crook St. goods warehouse. The Bridgeman St. warehouse is dimly visible in the distance. The crossover shown here was retained to allow excursion trains to have access to all platforms from the down line after removal of the up (Manchester) line further down the ramp. Prior to the re-signalling of the 1940's, a signal gantry spanned the tracks south of this crossover. The posts for the replacement individual signals can be seen on either side of the line. Photo, Author.

approximately the same position as the old, but was elevated with rails 10 feet above the level of Great Moor St., requiring trains to surmount a ramp with an upward gradient of 1 in 200 that commenced just after the entrance to the Crook St. yard at Fletcher St., and changed to a drop of 1 in 300 alongside the new Bolton No. 1 signal box, located to the east of the line as it crossed Crook St. by bridge. At the same time, the general level of the line around the area of Fletcher St. was raised, thus permitting some easing of the gradient of the bottom part of the Daubhill incline to 1 in 37, and Bolton No. 2 box was built to replace the original box demolished to make way for the ramp to the new station. The new Bolton No. 2 box was built facing the connection with the single line incline to Daubhill, and was presumably finished before the station signal box, Bolton No. 1, as No. 2 represents a classic example of the Saxby and Farmer Type 1 box, whereas

Bolton No. 1 is a very early example of a standard L&NWR design. Saxby and Farmer supplied signalling equipment to the L&NWR until 1874, after which the railway company took responsibility for its own signalling infrastructure. Bolton No. 1 box thus represented a transition period in signal box design on the L&NWR, and when demolished was one of the few examples of its type still in existence. Bolton No. 2 box was often referred to in official documents as Fletcher St. Jn., although the nameboard on the box was the former.

Early plans for the station at Great Moor Street, dated 1869 and presently in the local history collection of the Bolton library, show a covered facility with four tracks but only platform faces only on the outer two, whereas the station as built was wider, still with only four covered tracks but with the addition of a central island platform, thus providing platform faces for all four lines. A double

Plate 12. The exterior of Rumworth & Daubhill station in L&NWR days. The entrance to the station was located at road level at the north-west corner of the junction of St. Helens Road and Dean Church Lane. In this view, St. Helens Road runs left to right, and the tramlines down the centre of the road can just be seen.

Photo, Tillotsons.

20

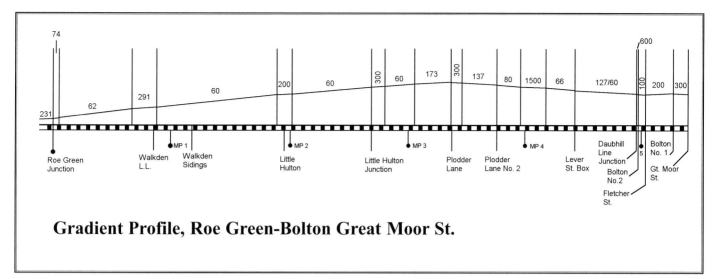

Gradient Profile, Roe Green-Bolton Great Moor St.

line of elevated coal drops, officially described as a 'coal viaduct', was built adjacent to the station on the east side and served as the Hulton Collieries outlet in Bolton, the coal being moved to Gt. Moor St. by carting it northwards under the tracks. When this new facility was brought into use, the older Hulton Collieries yard located at ground level across Gt. Moor St. was closed. Three shorter sidings were also built adjacent to the passenger station and served as the yard for the Fletcher-Burrows Collieries at Atherton. Coal was discharged from the latter sidings into a lower level coal yard, accessible by road, next to St. Patrick's school; these coal drops were particularly advantageous and remained in use in a modified form until 1965, long after the demise of passenger facilities.

The facilities of the new station were extensive, including the usual staff amenities together with waiting and refreshment rooms for passengers at platform level. The centre island platform was extended in length at an unknown date between 1882 and 1891, and the track layout was simplified by the removal of two short engine sidings at the platform ends. The station roof was cut back to about one half of its original length in 1930/31, and the signalling was renewed, it is thought during the 1940's. At this time a signal gantry spanning the passenger ramp was replaced by individual signal posts for the up and down lines, and the starting signals at the platform end, originally of L&NWR design on two brackets, were replaced by standard LM&SR signals on individual posts. Brick-built air raid shelters were provided on Platforms 1 and 4 during the second world war, but otherwise Bolton Great Moor Street station remained remarkably unchanged throughout its working life.

Gradient Profiles,
Fletcher St.- Deansgate and
High St.-Fletcher St.

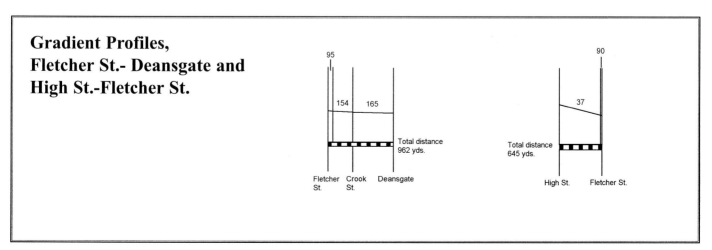

Plate 13. An unusual photograph of the platforms at Rumworth & Daubhill station, looking towards Bolton. The occasion cannot be identified, but perhaps cleaning of the station buildings was of sufficient interest to warrant the attentions of a photographer. The staff uniforms and station signs suggest a date prior to 1923.   Photo, Tillotsons.

Prior to and during construction of the Little Hulton Extension Railway, the goods facilities at Crook St. in Bolton were considerably expanded, including the provision of a new central three-storey warehouse with four covered roads that could be shunted by hydraulically powered capstans, a travelling crane and several stationary swivel-jib cranes, one with 20 tons lifting capacity, and a large network of new sidings linked by wagon turntables.   When the new warehouse was opened the original building alongside Crook St. was converted from a cotton warehouse to stables and offices, and the building on Chandos St. designated as a fruit and vegetable warehouse. The cattle dock and holding pens in the Crook St. yard were also built at this time.

Plate 14. The road entrance to Crook St. goods yard on 7th. December 1963, through one of the original warehouses on the site that predated the Crook St. expansion of the 1870's. The painted signs on the wall on either side of the gate read "Phillip Thomas & Co. Ltd., Coal and Coke Merchants," and the later BR signs, in maroon enamel, inform the visitor "DISTRICT GOODS MANAGER'S OFFICE CENTRALISED ACCOUNTS SECTION THROUGH ARCH AND TURN LEFT".
Photo, Author.

THE BOLTON AND LEIGH LINE REBUILT

In the late 1870's and early 1880's the decision was made to reconstruct much of the Atherton to Bolton section as double track, to by-pass the incline from Bolton to Daubhill by construction of a new line to the south of the original, and to re-align the incline between Chequerbent and Atherton on a more westerly location that allowed for a slight easing of the gradient. New stations were built at Daubhill (now named Rumworth and Daubhill) to replace the original building located north of Adelaide Street and now to be devoid of any rail connection, and at Chequerbent. Rumworth and Daubhill station was located on the new line at the junction of St. Helens Road and Deane Church Lane, just east of the junction with the original route, and the new route was opened throughout in 1885. A 250 yard tunnel, whose northerly portal was adjacent to the entrance to the tunnel of the Manchester line, was necessary at the Bolton end. Both ends of the original single track formation of the Daubhill incline were retained; that from Bolton ran as far as High St., where a coal depot was established, and from 1902 also served a siding at the Crown (later Magee, Marshall's) brewery, while the western end of the original route was retained from a junction west of the new Daubhill station to serve one coal depot at Daubhill, and another adjacent to the large complex at Sunnyside Mills on Adelaide Street. The northern end of the Chequerbent incline was also retained to serve the Chequerbent and Bank collieries. Bolton No. 2 signal box was retained in its location at the junction of the original route to Daubhill, but the new line now diverged from the Manchester route at a double track junction south of the site of the original junction and signal box. The original junction thus became redundant for through trains, but since the signal box had been built facing this junction it was now 'back to front' with respect to the new junction it was to serve for the next 60 years.

Plate 15. The interior view that would face a passenger alighting from a Manchester train at Platform 3 of Bolton Gt. Moor St. station. The railings guard the staircase that leads down to the booking hall and the exit at street level. To the left of the staircase, the etched glass windows in the door proclaim the Ladies Waiting Room, while the double doors to the right lead to office accommodation. Although taken on 7th. December 1963, almost ten years after closure to regular passenger traffic, the interior of the station is in good condition, with all the glass intact, and looks like the next train is due shortly.

Photo, Author.

THE LITTLE HULTON ROUTE DESCRIBED

There were no passenger facilities at Roe Green, the infrastructure consisting only of a signal box and long siding parallel with down (Wigan and Bolton) line approaching the junction from the Manchester direction. The Little Hulton line left the direct Wigan line on a tangent, the latter curving to the west whereas the branch line proceeded straight towards Walkden. Up trains from Bolton to Manchester had an easy passage, but down trains had to cross the up Wigan line before gaining access to the branch, preventing a run at the gradient of 1 in 62 which began immediately after the junction. A climb of almost a mile at 1 in 62 on straight track brought the train to Walkden station, where a brief easing of the gradient to 1 in 291 made the starting of down trains for Bolton less problematic. The station was built in a cutting, and consisted of brick-built facilities on both up and down lines, reached by ramps from the adjacent roadway. There were no goods facilities or signal box at Walkden station; immediately after leaving the station the L&NWR line passed under a road bridge, and then under the L&YR tracks from Manchester to Wigan (Wallgate), whereupon the gradient reverted to a climb 1 in 60 towards Bolton.

A further 1/4 mile brought the line to Walkden Sidings, where the Bridgewater Colliery line from Mosley Common to Ashtons Field crossed overhead and a connection from the colliery system trailed in on the down (west) side of the line, opposite the site of Walkden Sidings signal box, to enter a set of exchange sidings. Walkden was otherwise devoid of any goods facilities on the L&NWR line. As the line continued to climb at 1 in 60, a short-lived facing connection with Smith Fold colliery, removed within a decade of construction, was passed on the down side immediately prior to reaching Little Hulton station, again built without goods facilities or signal box, and sited in a cutting on a brief stretch of line inclined upwards at 1 in 300. Immediately upon leaving that station the gradient reverted to 1 in 60 for a further 3/4 mile to Little Hulton Junction, where the mineral branch trailed in on the down side. At the junction itself, a signal box was located between the down line and the branch, facing the former. The original formation included only a trailing crossover on the through lines, and a trap point on the branch, but a long siding parallel to the down line, reaching northwards from the junction to Spa Lane, was added at a later date.

Plate 16. The 5-ton capacity hand crane in the goods yard at Plodder lane on 21st. July 1964, still functional but probably never to be used again. The products of the 1930's housing developments to the east of the yard can be seen in the background.

Photo, Author.

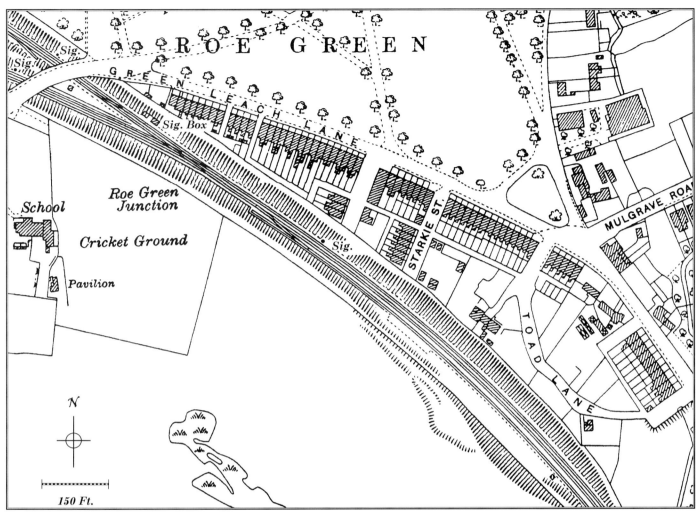

Roe Green Jn., c1930

The line to Little Hulton and Bolton diverges from the through route to Wigan at Roe Green Jn. signal box. The long siding on the down side of the through line is visible, and at the southern extremity of this map is the terminus of the four-road yard at Sanderson's Siding.

Plate 17. The Highfield Sidings ground frame in October 1951, a standard LNWR size 'A' design, but built by the LM&SR in replacement of an earlier version. The size of the building may have dictated the singular version of the name used on the board   Photo, Harry Jack.

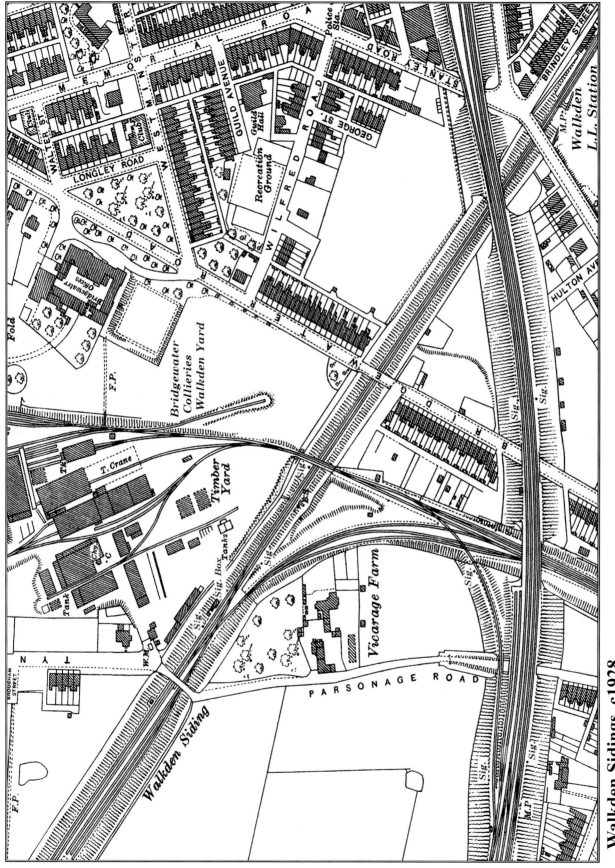

Walkden Sidings, c1928.

With the low level passenger station in the south-east corner, the L&NWR line passes underneath the L&YR route from Manchester to Wigan and the Bridgewater Collieries line from Mosley Common to Ashtons Field as it approaches Walkden Sidings. The interchange facilities with the L&NWR route at Walkden were not extensive: the connection between the Colliery system and the L&YR route is also shown, as are the extensive locomotive workshops and other facilities of the former at Walkden Yard.

Plate 18. The goods shed at Plodder Lane, seen from the south end with the running lines in the foreground on 21st. July 1964. Although nominally still in use at this time, the shed had been the subject of an arson attack and the windows of the office area were boarded up. Photo, Author.

Plate 19. The approach to Plodder Lane from the Bolton direction on 21st. July 1964. The goods shed is on the left, with the Plodder Lane overbridge in the distance. The site of the engine sheds is to the right of the photographer, and the footpath or 'ginnel' that led from Plodder Lane to the sheds can be identified by the row of sleeper fencing running down from the road. The shed entrance was the gate in this fencing on the extreme right of the photograph. Photo, Author.

A trip down the Little Hulton Mineral Branch, which was single track once the immediate area of the junction was passed, would, at the time of construction, have led to connections with no less than seven coal mines in the space of just over one mile, the pits concerned being (in order from the junction), Bank Colliery, Peel Colliery, New Watergate Colliery, Peel Hall Colliery, New Lester Colliery, Wharton Hall Colliery, and Charlton Colliery. In later years an end-on junction with the Bridgewater Collieries railway system also allowed access to Brackley Colliery, and in 1904 Edward Bennis & Co. (Engineers) took over the connection to the Bank Colliery, closed in 1884.

Back on the Bolton line, down trains leaving Little Hulton Junction began to climb again at 1 in 60, and emerged from a long cutting onto an embankment which ran as far as Highfield Road (Farnworth). In this section the single track of the colliery branch, opened around 1908, that served the Dixon Green landsale yard at the bottom of Highfield Road was crossed on an overbridge that would become notorious after the second world war for the murder of a schoolboy, Quentin Smith, under the western side of its arch. Just south of the Highfield Road overbridge, Highfield Sidings were located on the up (east) side of the L&NWR line. Under an agreement with the Earl of Bradford, the original sidings were installed some time after the opening of the line in 1874, but prior to 1891, and additional siding facilities and a ground frame were built to serve the Scowcroft coal depot on Highfield road at a later date, certainly before 1909. Scowcrofts took over responsibility for the sidings in 1917. In connection with the expansion of Highfield Sidings, the up distant signal, the post for which also carried the up starting signal for Plodder Lane station, was re-sited from its original position close to Highfield ground frame to a new location adjacent to Highfield Road, necessitating a tall installation that carried the signals well above the level of the Highfield Road bridge.

The approach to Highfield Sidings from the south was marked by an easing of the climb from 1 in 60

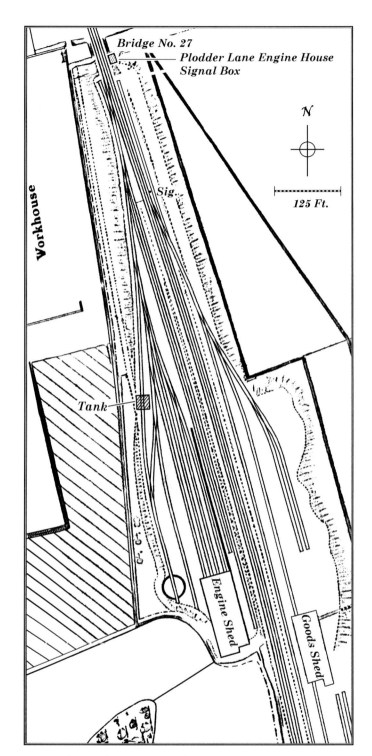

Plodder Lane, c1876.

The original layout of Plodder Lane sheds, showing the four-road shed close to the running lines, with the turntable and water tank on the opposite side of the shed yard. The description of Plodder Lane No. 2 signal box as the 'Engine House Signal Box' is taken verbatim from the original plan.

to 1 in 173, the latter gradient continuing to the summit of the line at Plodder Lane station where the gradient post was located in the centre of the down platform. In just over 3¼ miles from Roe Green Junction the line had climbed a total of 210 feet, and was to fall another 60 feet in the next 1¾ miles to a low point underneath Fletcher Street in Bolton, prior to climbing the ramp to Great Moor Street station. Also present on the east (up) side of the line between Little Hulton and Highfield Sidings ground frame were a series of white posts, six feet in height and marked with heights above rail level in feet and 6" intervals, that were intended to monitor possible subsidence of the ground cause by colliery workings below ground level.

Just before entering Plodder Lane station the line passed over bridge 24, spanning the site of a former sandstone quarry. Plodder Lane station was, like Walkden and Little Hulton, located in a cutting, being accessible from Plodder Lane via the road-level booking office and an open wooden footbridge across the tracks, but unlike the other two stations which were of brick construction, the station at Plodder Lane was finished in horizontal wooden planking. Both up and down sides had a general waiting room, the down side being equipped with a urinal at the southern end and the up line having separate gentleman's and ladies facilities.

Through the station and immediately north of the Plodder Lane overbridge, Plodder Lane No.1, an early example of the L&NWR standard gable D size signal box, was located on the up side of the line at the end of the trap points guarding the southern entrance to the goods yard. This box had controlled a crossover in the station area that was removed about 1900, and a starter and home signal on the down line that were both removed at a later date. No.1 box found little use thereafter, apart from controlling the southern access to the goods yard and releasing the ground frame at Highfield Sidings. In later years the up line signals at the station remained permanently in the

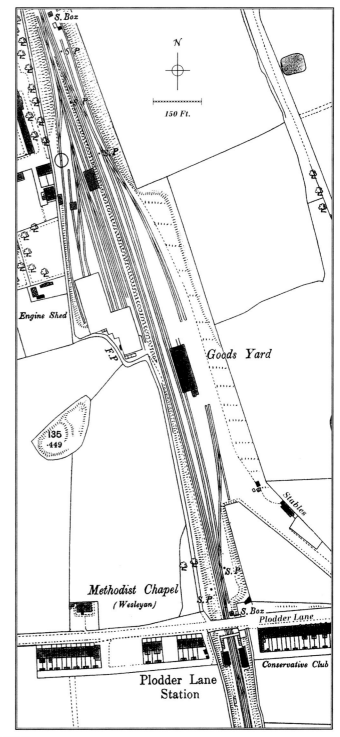

Plodder Lane, c1891. The new six-road shed adjoining the original four-road building is present, but the lines into the new shed are incomplete and, although the new water tank/coaling stage is shown, the original water tank is still in situ. The turntable had been moved to a new location, but the alterations to the shed are clearly incomplete at this time. Other features to note are the existence of a headshunt at the southern end of the goods yard, the presence of the trailing crossover in the station, and a signal controlling the down (Bolton) line just north of the Plodder Lane bridge.

'on' position. The spacious goods yard with its 5 ton capacity crane was laid out on the up side, and had two through roads (one of which passed through the two-storey goods shed), and four additional sidings, two from each of the north and south ends. As the line dropped past the goods shed, the engine sheds were located on the down side adjacent to the Bolton workhouse (later Townley's Hospital). Just before crossing the Minerva road bridge, Plodder Lane No. 2 signal box, a standard flat-gable size C box, and the northern entrance to the goods yard were located on the up side of the line, while the tracks from the engine shed trailed into the down line. Plodder Lane No. 2 thus controlled access to both the yard (from the northern end) and the engine sheds, and was by far the busier of the two signal boxes at Plodder Lane. The line continued to fall on an embankment until the Lever Edge Lane overbridge, where it entered a cutting to emerge from the Bridge Street bridge with Lever Street signal box on the down side, and the entrance to Lever Street yard, subject to a 15 mph speed restriction, on the up side of the line. The arrangements at Lever St. were simple, four sidings accessible from the up line and a crossover from the down line, and were laid out in a spacious area adjoining Rupert Street. When built the yard possessed an overhead gantry crane of 10 tons capacity spanning the two central sidings, almost certainly installed to handle cotton and timber traffic for the local mills, but this was removed prior to the 1930's after which only coal traffic was handled at Lever St.

Highfield Sidings, c1891

The reason for the singular description of 'Highfield Siding' used by the L&NWR is apparent from this early map: there was only one siding. The Plodder Lane station area is relatively undeveloped at this time, but note the trailing crossover between the platforms. This was controlled by No.1 signalbox (to the north of the Plodder Lane bridge).

Little Hulton Jn., c1929 (opposite)

Little Hulton Jn. was in an isolated location, surrounded by fields. The long siding running north to Spa Lane was not part of the original construction, but added at a later date for operating convenience. The mineral branch was single track beyond the loop shown here.

30

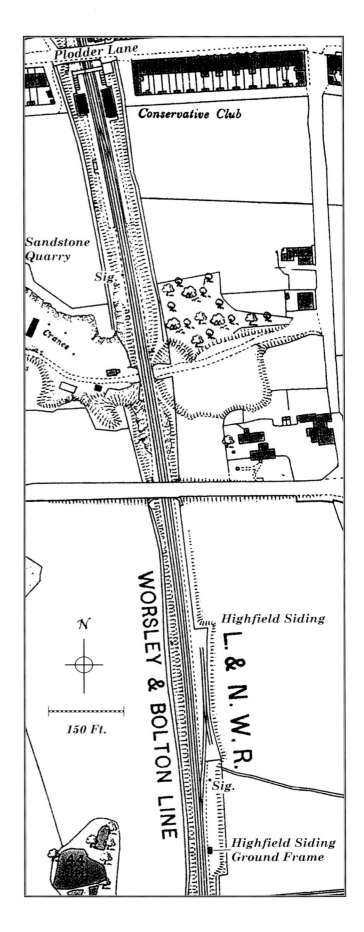

Plate 20. The entrance to Plodder Lane station on 18th.September 1955. Although closed for over a year, the building is in good condition. From Plodder Lane this building was all that was visible of the station.   Photo, Harry Jack.

Plate 21. (below) The bridge over Spa Road at Little Hulton Jn. in October 1951, looking north towards Plodder Lane. The signal is pure L&NWR, and as usual at this time was left permanently in the 'off' position. On the extreme left, the partially visible buffer stop marks the end of the siding that ran north from Little Hulton Jn. to terminate at the bridge. Just visible in front of the first telegraph pole beyond the bridge is a white subsidence marker post, once a common sight alongside railways in the coal mining areas of Lancashire.   Photo, Harry Jack.

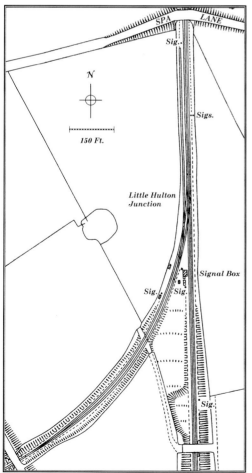

Once Lever Street yard was passed, the line entered a short tunnel beneath the Bolton recreation grounds, to emerge underneath Bridgeman Street. Before the construction of the new line to Daubhill, the line from Manchester continued alone until Fletcher Street Junction, where Bolton No. 2 signal box was located on the down side and the single line from Daubhill joined the tracks from Manchester under Fletcher Street bridge and opposite the Atlas Forge. From 1885 the new double track connection from the Daubhill direction emerged from its own tunnel adjacent to that of the Manchester Line, and the junction with this line was passed before reaching No. 2 box.

Emerging from underneath the Fletcher Street bridge, passenger trains would take the ramp on the east side of the railway property, climbing past the Soho Foundry to pass Bolton No. 1 box on the up side at Crook St. on their way to the terminus. Trains from Manchester would arrive at platform 3 (the second most easterly) and depart from platform 4 (the furthest east), platforms 1 and 2 being used for trains from the Atherton direction. Goods trains did not use the station ramp, taking the more westerly lines into Crook Street yard.

Highfield Sidings, c1929

By this time Highfield Sidings had been expanded to assume their final arrangement, terminating in the yard alongside Highfield Road. The close proximity of the Conservative Club close to the station is apparent. Note also the relocation of the up signal to a position closer to Highfield Road than that shown in the 1891 map.

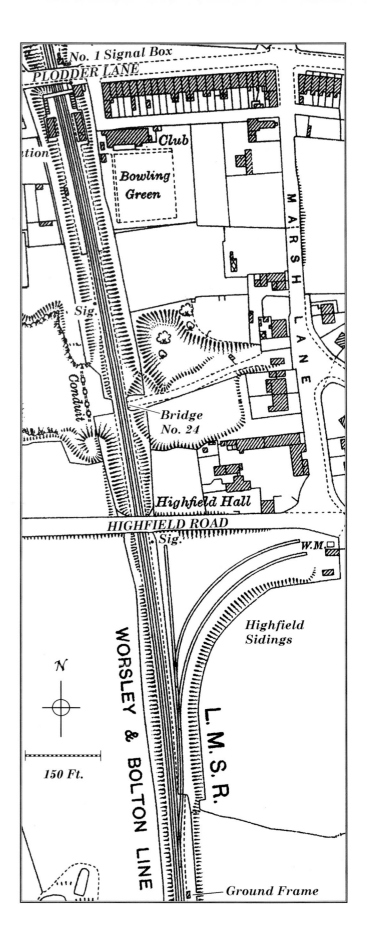

THE LATER ROUTE FROM BOLTON
TO ATHERTON

Leaving Bolton for the Atherton and Leigh direction, passengers trains proceeded from Gt. Moor St. station past Bolton No. 1 signal box, gave three short whistles to the signalman into let him know they were taking the Kenyon direction (two short whistles signified the Little Hulton line), and then ran down the ramp from Great Moor Street station, observing the 20 mph speed restriction over the junctions at Fletcher Street, Trains for the Kenyon direction followed the Manchester route past Bolton No. 2 signal box at Fletcher St. before diverging to the west shortly after passing the box and just after passing beneath Rothwell Street. The line then immediately entered a tunnel, again beneath the Bolton recreation grounds, and emerged climbing at 1 in 60 on a gentle but continuous curve to the west that would last until Rumworth & Daubhill station was reached.

The small covered ground frame controlling Townson's siding (serving a contractor's and wood yard) was passed on the south (down) side of the line before reaching Rumworth and Daubhill station, a gloomy affair with a road-level booking office, the platforms being located in a cutting and each reached from St. Helens road by sets of covered

steps. The buildings at platform level were quite extensive, incorporating a canopy on both up and down sides. Leaving the station, the junction with the remaining southern end of the original Bolton and Leigh line, located on the north or up (towards Bolton) side of the new formation, was passed just before the signal box at Rumworth & Daubhill, the latter located on the north side of the line. The small yard at Daubhill on the original formation was known officially by the L&NWR as Engine House Sidings, presumably after the stationary engine used to power the incline in earlier days, although this engine had not been located where the yard was built, but was further north on the original formation closer to Adelaide St. The small yard at Daubhill was leased for many years to the Hulton Colliery Company and constituted the only goods facilities at Rumworth & Daubhill, although the original formation was retained to a point close to the original Daubhill station on Adelaide St. where a substantial yard for coal traffic incorporating two double lines of coal drops was laid out adjacent to the Sunnyside Mills.

The summit of the new line was passed shortly after leaving Rumworth & Daubhill, from which a gentle

Plate 22. A view of Chequerbent incline, looking south, clearly showing the effects of subsidence on the gradient. The steepest part of the incline was just to the north (camera side) of the bridge shown. The step in the embankment on the left marks the course of the original Bolton and Leigh line, already higher than the deviation route at this point. 22nd. July 1967.
Photo, J. Marshall.

33

descent at 1 in 425 took the tracks past Hulton Sidings and Chequerbent before the drop to Atherton began in earnest. Hulton Sidings signal box was located at Pendlebury Fold on the up side of the line, and was a busy box, controlling entry to a number of sidings. Of these, the longest stretched from the down side of the main line to Booth's steel works, located on St. Helens Road in Bolton, and on the same side of the line another set of sidings controlled entry to several of the Hulton collieries, at one time serving the Arley, Arley Deep and School pits. On the up side, a siding which had once extended to Endless Chain Pit, but cut back prior to 1870 to serve only the Hulton brick works, trailed in from the west.

As the line continued to fall towards Chequerbent, the original course of the Bolton and Leigh Railway route diverged to the east. This single track formation continued in use as a private siding connection, serving Chequerbent Nos. 1 and 2 pits and other collieries, and is thought to have survived until 1934 in this capacity. Approaching the contemporary station on the new formation, Chequerbent goods yard was located on the up (Bolton) side of the line, and the signal box situated across from the yard entrance on the down side, just off the end of the platform.

From Chequerbent to Atherton the new line dropped 200 feet in 1.6 miles, but the gradient was not the uniform 1 in 30.5 originally surveyed. Mining subsidence over the years led to an uneven profile, claimed to contain a short section as steep as

1 in 18. Careful assessment of Ordnance Survey spot heights and contemporary photographs, using the positions of two overbridges and the site of the bridge carrying the L&NWR line over the L&Y Manchester-Wigan route as markers, together with observations of gradient posts along the route in 1963, has led to the gradient profile shown here, which includes a short section of approximately 1 in 18 underneath the southernmost overbridge. A triangular junction on the west side of incline, 1114 yards north of Atherton station and approximately in the centre of the 1 in 30.5 portion, was installed around 1900 and led to the Pretoria and Bank pits but this connection, which was very difficult to work, especially in the Bolton direction up the incline, was taken out and the colliery line removed prior to 1934. A signal box to control this connection, Chequerbent Bank Box, was located alongside the up line just north of this junction, but was closed when the colliery line was disconnected.

Towards the bottom end of the incline the L&NWR route passed over the L&YR line, before a short section at 1 in 43 brought the former line down to Atherton, known as Atherton (Bag Lane) from 1924 to distinguish it from its former L&Y neighbour. Goods facilities at Bag Lane were extensive, including a private siding north of the station on the up (Bolton) side into the Urban District Council's yard, extensive holding sidings on the up side for traffic waiting for assistance up the incline to Chequerbent, and a yard incorporating a warehouse and a 10-ton capacity crane on the down side, just

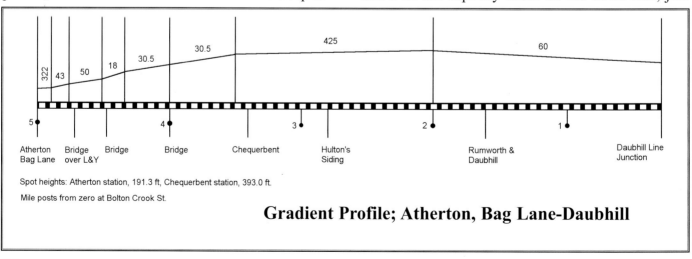

Spot heights: Atherton station, 191.3 ft, Chequerbent station, 393.0 ft.

Mile posts from zero at Bolton Crook St.

Gradient Profile; Atherton, Bag Lane-Daubhill

south of the passenger station. The goods yard at Atherton was directly connected to the Gibfield Colliery complex of lines on the down side, shortly following which Atherton Junction was reached, where lines diverted to the east and west junctions with the L&NWR Manchester - Wigan line at Howe Bridge, and the through line led to Pennington and Kenyon Jn.

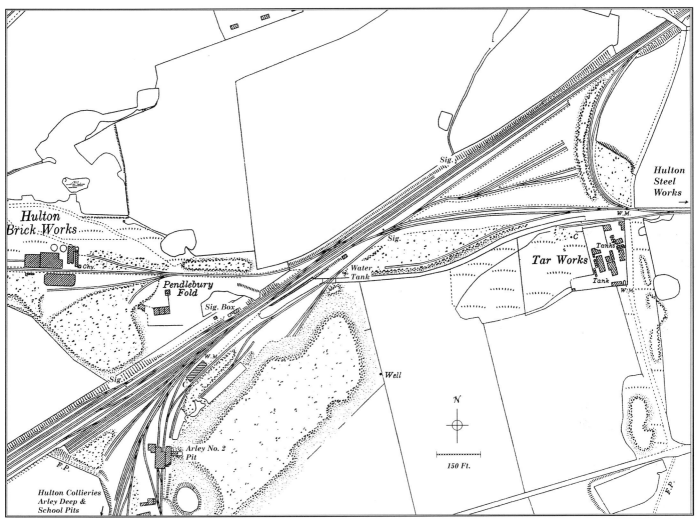

Hulton Sidings c1930.

The location of Hulton Sidings signal box at Pendlebury Fold was ideal for controlling traffic to and from the various locations shown on this map. Although central from a railway point of view, the signal box was in a isolated location, which explains its role as a social centre for engine crews working the Atherton banking engines and trips along the branch lines from Hulton Sidings. Although there appears to be three running lines here, the southernmost of the three is the original formation of the Bolton and Leigh Railway and does not continue beyond the bridge in the north-east corner. Heading towards the south-west, it was soon to deviate from the double track formation as the lines neared Chequerbent.

Chequerbent, c1930.

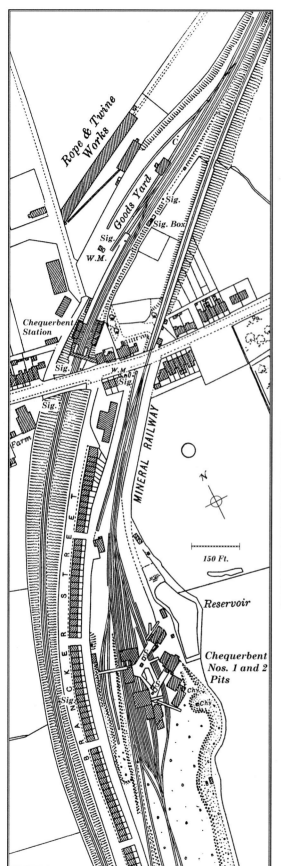

The new double track deviation line to the left of the original single track Bolton and Leigh formation are both clearly shown. At this point in time the latter was still used to serve Chequerbent Nos. 1 and 2 pits (shown), and the Bank pits (further to the south). The top of the incline from Atherton was situated under the road bridge just to the south of the new Chequerbent station. The original Chequerbent station and sidings were located to the south of the point where the original single track crossed the road on the level.

Plate 23. Stanier 8F No.48491 is seen working hard at the head of a freight train from Bag Lane, Atherton, comprising 12 vehicles including the brake van, bound for Hulton Sidings about 1964. Such a short load as this would not need the banker as seen in evidence here on other parts of the system but the severity of the incline clearly shows in this photograph. Unfortunately the banker is unidentified.

The waste tips of Hulton Colliery's Bank Pits stand testamount to the heavy mining activity once prevalent in this area. The mills of Atherton form the backdrop to the scene.

Photo, Alex Mann.

In addition to the facilities mentioned above, a considerable number of private and railway company sidings were connected to the railway system in the Roe Green-Bolton-Atherton triangle, and thus came within the sphere of workings from Plodder Lane. At the most easterly end of the area under consideration, the Sanderson's siding interchange with the Bridgewater Collieries system was located on the Manchester side of Roe Green Junction, and handled interchange traffic both from the colliery system and the Bridgewater canal. The interchange facilities with the colliery railway system at Walkden have already been mentioned, as have the yards at Highfield Sidings, and Plodder Lane.

The Lever Street yard in Bolton was owned exclusively by the L&NWR, but was leased in part to the Astley & Tyldesley Colliery Co. from 1888 until 1914. Over the years, a number of smaller coal merchants also occupied space at Lever St., including Samuel Kershaw & Sons, Adam Kay, W.N. Birchby, James Lomax, Jonathan Welsby (in the 1920's), John Hilton & Sons (in the early 1930's), and I.Tomlinson (in the 1950's). The Anglo-American Oil Co., who had premises at Bridgeman St. in Bolton, were also located in the Lever St. yard from 1894, but had vacated their premises there by the 1920's.

The Crook Street goods complex in Bolton was the site of much shunting and transfer activity involving both company and private sidings. In addition to the maze of sidings in the immediate Crook St. area, the branch to Deansgate, dating from 1829, ran across Crook St. on the level and then along Ormrod Street, passing through the steel works complex and serving a small coal yard before crossing Railway Street to reach its destination in the warehouse on Deansgate. The remnants of the Bolton and Leigh route provided termini at High St. and Adelaide St., both used as coal yards, in addition to serving sidings for Crown (Magee Marshall's) Brewery at the Bolton end and the Hulton collieries at Daubhill.

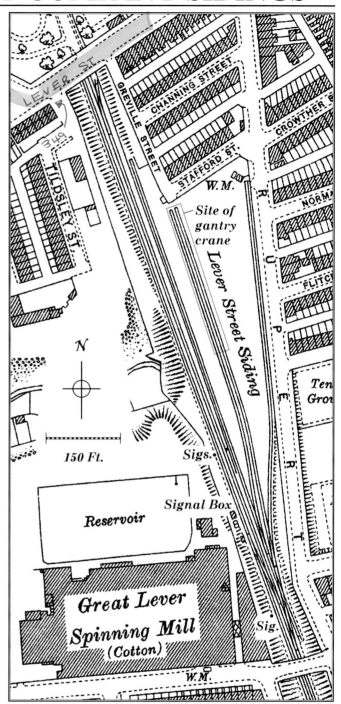

Lever St. Yard, c1929.

Although surrounded by terraced housing to the north and west, Lever St. yard had ample space for the traffic on offer. The central two roads were once spanned by a gantry crane, probably for unloading cotton traffic for the nearby mills, but this had been removed by 1929.

Plate 24. Facing south from Fletcher St. bridge in Bolton , three sets of lines are seen. The building on the left is part of the Atlas Forge, extended to cover part of the private sidings in a unique manner that made the most of the available space. The running lines to Plodder Lane and Atherton diverge to the left to pass Bolton No. 2 signal box, while the single track on the right is the original Bolton and Leigh formation on its way to the High St. terminus.

Photo, J.Jones

The full list of private sidings and rail-served facilities in the Crook St. area is extensive, and with changes in names and location over the years, the story is also complex. For the purposes of tabulation it is best divided geographically, distinguishing those concerns which were rail-connected from those which only possessed buildings or yard equipment without having a private siding agreement with the railway company. The following information is consistent with that contained in a copy of the L&NWR Private Sidings Diagram Book, itself undated but containing the dates of siding diagrams and details of the dates of siding agreements.

The Deansgate branch:

In addition to the Deansgate warehouse itself, the following sidings were located along this branch:

1. Bessemer's Moore (sic) Lane Siding, located immediately south and west of the Deansgate warehouse. This was used by a local contractor, J.W. Pollitt, from 1881, then became a coal yard, leased by James Roscoe from 1888 to 1902, and the Astley & Tyldesley Colliery Co. until 1914, at which time it was taken over by Bessemer's Steel for their own use.

2. Bolton Steel Works Siding (formerly the Bolton Forge and Union Foundry), a complex of eight sidings on both sides of the branch in the steelworks area. This was taken over by Bessemer's in 1907 and run by them until closure in 1924.

The Great Moor Street station area:

1. Fletcher Burrows Coal Yard Siding, adjacent to the ground-level yard on Dawes St., east of Gt. Moor St. station.

2. Hulton Co.'s Moor St. Yard Siding, occupying the coal drops immediately adjacent to Gt. Moor St. station. These sidings closed in 1936.

The Bridgeman Street area: (Crook Street yard, east of the ramp to the passenger station):

1. Albion Cane Works, on the corner of Fletcher St. and Bridgeman Street, to the east of Victoria Mill, was not rail connected. It was used as a store by the Royal Navy from 1950 to 1955.

2. British Petroleum, Shell-Mex and the Anglo-American Oil Co. (later Esso Petroleum), whose plant was located north of the Bridgeman Street warehouse from 1919, was not directly rail connected but received tank wagons of oil and petroleum products by rail, using the Bridgeman St. warehouse sidings. Prior to 1919 the Anglo-American Oil Co. also had an office in Lever St. yard.

3. Hargreaves Victoria Mill Siding, adjacent to the mill in the south east corner of the Crook St. area.

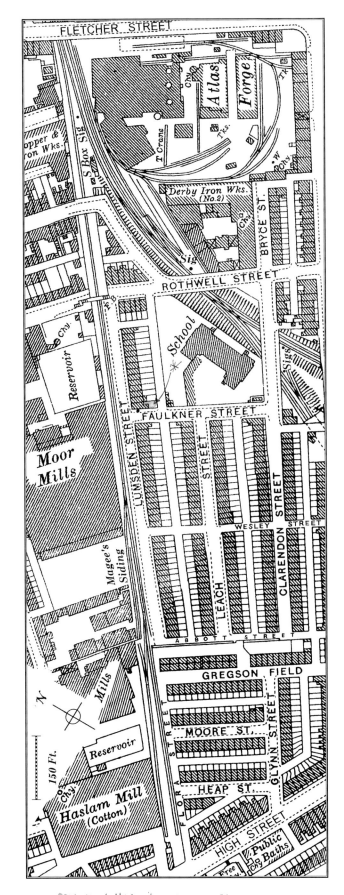

FLETCHER STREET

Atlas Forge

Copper & Iron Wks.

S Box Sig.

Derby Iron Wks. (No.2)

BRYCE ST.

Sig.

ROTHWELL STREET

Reservoir

School

Moor Mills

FAULKNER STREET

LUMSDEN STREET

LEACH STREET

CLARENDON STREET

WESLEY STREET

Magee's Siding

Mills

ABBOTT STREET

GREGSON FIELD

N

150 Ft.

Reservoir

MOORE ST.

FLORA STREET

GLYNN STREET

HEAP ST.

Haslam Mill (Cotton)

HIGH STREET

Public Baths

*MICK HARAN'S HOUSE 1968

Magee's Siding and High St. Yard, c1930

In conjunction with the map of the Crook St. area in 1930, this map shows almost the full extent of the former L&NWR operations in Bolton. The single line leading past Magee's siding to the High St. yard is seen diverting from the through running lines at Fletcher St., with Bolton No. 2 signal box in the angle of the two routes, and the divergence of the Atherton and Little Hulton routes at a double track junction just south of Rothwell St. is clearly shown. The extent of the sidings at the Atlas Forge required the use of at least one, and sometimes two private shunting engines at this location.

Victoria Mill was disconnected from the railway between 1887 and 1898 when it was owned by William Rothwell (hosiery manufacturers), but then reconnected after being bought by the L&NWR and put into use as their Bridgeman Street Goods warehouse in 1900, as such bringing additional shunting requirements to the area. It was extended on the south side by the L&NWR in 1902. J. Walker (Iron & Steel) used the 1902 extension to the warehouse from 1953 to 1967.

4. Hulton Co.'s Coal Yard Sidings, located at the south eastern side of the Crook St. complex adjacent to The Soho Foundry. This yard was built by the Hulton Co. but not used by them after 1875 when their new coal drops adjacent to Gt. Moor St. station were brought into use. It was leased to J. Briggs & Son for use as a coal yard from 1887. Briggs were agents for (among others) the Abram Coal Co., Bickershaw Collieries, and the Atherton and Hulton Collieries.

5. Soho Iron Works Siding, owned by Hick, Hargreaves & Co., located on the eastern side of the railway property adjacent to the ramp to Great Moor St. station.

Crook Street yard, west of the ramp to the passenger station:

1. The Buxton Lime Co., occupying a small yard to the west of Chandos Street from 1861 to 1901. Between 1901 and 1919 this yard was used by a number of coal merchants, and in 1919 was taken over by Thomas Walmsley and the land used for expansion of their warehouse.

2. Thomas Walmsley's warehouse, located on the west side of Chandos Street. This was extended in 1919 to take over the site of the Buxton Lime Co.'s

39

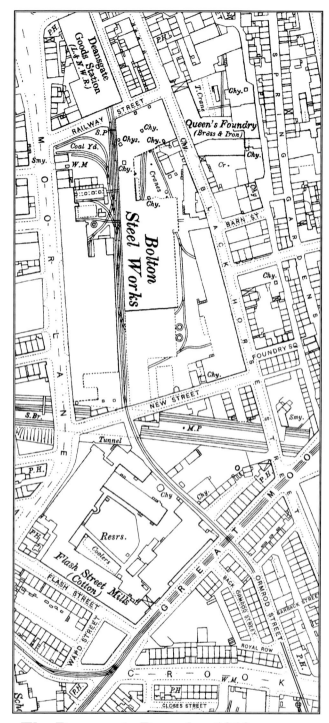

The Deansgate Branch, c1910.

In 1910 the Bolton Steel Works occupies the area between Moor Lane and Blackhorse St., and is served by the Deansgate branch, which crosses Crook St. at bottom right, proceeds along Ormrod St. to cross the L&YR tracks before entering the steelworks complex. The branch terminates in the Deansgate warehouse. Immediately to the south of Railway St. is the coal yard leased by Pollitt's and then James Roscoe & Co.

yard, and later sold to Bolton Corporation for use as a bus garage, designed as their C depot before being taken over for the same purposes by the Greater Manchester Passenger Transport Board.

3. Bolton Corporation bus garage alongside Chandos Street (previously Thomas Walmsley's warehouse), was rail connected by 1932 and remained so into the 1950's.

4. J. Booth & Co. (Booth's Steel, with a connection from Hulton Sidings as noted above) also had a siding in the Fletcher Street area at an unknown date, thought to have been located with the Astley & Tyldesley Colliery Sidings in the south west corner of Crook St. yard behind the cattle dock.

5. Thomas Mitchell Engineering, located at the western edge of the Crook St. area, dealers in locomotives and engineering machinery, were not directly rail-connected but are known to have occasionally rented sidings in the Crook St. area when needed for locomotive storage.

6. The Hulmes Charity Trustees Sidings: the Trustees of the Hulmes Charity owned all the land west of Chandos Street, and over the years a large number of lessees had siding accommodation in this area. From 1875 to 1915 the facilities consisted of three small yards, one to the west of what was known as 'Little Crook St'., and two to the east. These were used by John Scowcroft & Co. (Hindley Green Collieries), the Wharton Hall Colliery Co., The Bridgewater Trustees, E.R. Johnson (colliery agents for the principal collieries in Little Hulton, Wigan and other districts) from 1890 to 1900, and William Ramsden & Sons (Shakerley Colliery, Tyldesley). In 1914 a new yard was built south of the existing facilities and on land immediately to the west of the cattle dock. This was for the Astley & Tyldesley Collieries Ltd., who moved there from the Lever St. yard. In 1915 the three older yards were remodelled into two yards. The westerly one continued to be used by William Ramsden until the early 1920's, after which it was used by the Bolton Co-operative Society (later the Co-operative Wholesale Society) for coal traffic, and the easterly one by the Bridgewater Collieries.

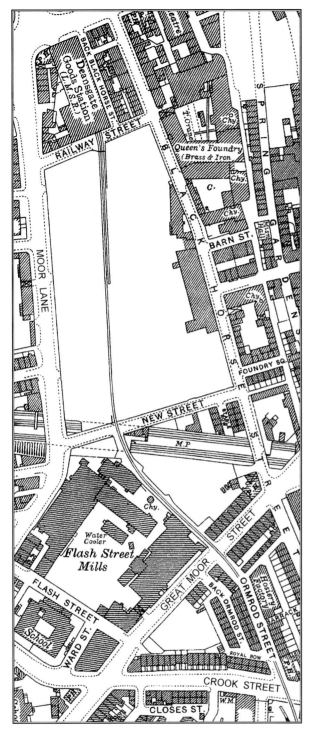

The Deansgate Branch, c1930.

The Bolton steel works closed in 1924 and by 1930 the area had been cleared, but the branch still ran across the site of steel works to serve Deansgate warehouse until closure of the latter in 1930.

Crook Street, outside the immediate yard area:

Atlas Iron Works Siding, located at the entrance to the Atlas Forge on the south side of Fletcher St. bridge. The Atlas Iron Works were owned by Thomas Walmsley, whose warehouse was located on Chandos St. In spite of Atlas Works having its own locomotives, the traffic between there and the warehouse was handled exclusively by the railway company.

At a greater distance from the Crook St. yard, but still in the local vicinity, the following sidings were shunted on a regular basis:

1. Crown Brewery Siding (later Magee, Marshall's siding), built in 1902 on west side the Bolton and Leigh route between Fletcher Street and the High Street yard, continued in use until 1964.

2. High St. Coal Yard, at the terminus of the Bolton and Leigh Railway route from Bolton, used by the Wigan Coal and Iron Co. from 1890 until the 1930's, closed to coal traffic in 1947 but was used by Watson's Steelworks from the late 1930's to the 1950's, perhaps later.

3. W. Townson's Siding, located alongside Upper Swan Lane on the new line from Bolton to Daubhill.

4. Hulton Colliery Co.'s Sidings (Engine House Siding), located on the original Bolton and Leigh formation at Daubhill.

5. Adelaide Street Sidings (Sunnyside Mill), located at the truncated terminus of the Bolton and Leigh route from Daubhill. This yard was used by John Scowcroft & Co. (Hindley Green Collieries) until the 1920's, then briefly by Albert Greenhalgh (Colliery Agent), and was occupied by Philip Thomas (Coal Agent) from the 1950's.

Further along the line towards Atherton, the sidings at Hulton Sidings (Hulton Brick Works, Hulton Steel (Booth's Steel) and later the Hilton Gravel Co. siding), Chequerbent (the Chequerbent and Hulton Collieries), and Atherton (Fletcher's Gibfield colliery and the UDC siding) have already been mentioned in the previous section.

Although the larger concerns in Bolton (Bolton Steel Works and the Atlas Forge) possessed their own shunting locomotives for internal use, transfer duties and the remainder of the shunting work was the responsibility of the L&NWR and its successors, and will be discussed in Chapter 4.

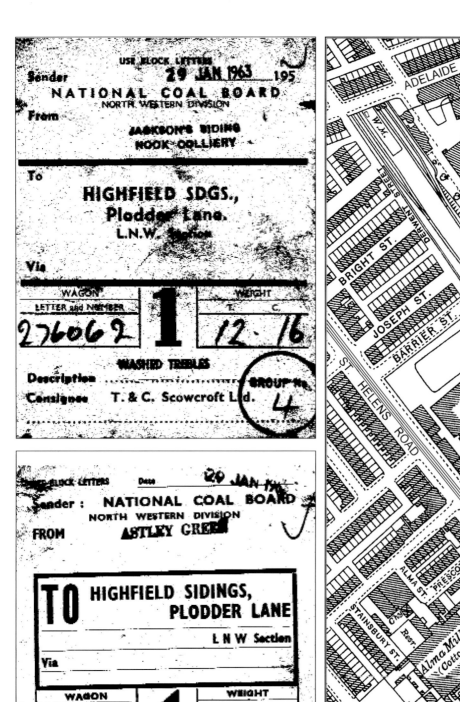

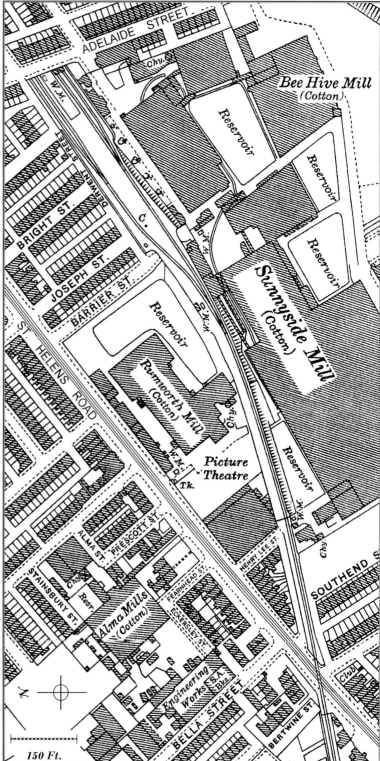

Sunnyside Mills, Adelaide St. yard, c1930

The line from Daubhill crossed the tramlines on St. Helens Road to terminate in the coal yard on the west side of Adelaide St. This map suggests that Sunnyside and Beehive Mills may have had an internal railway system, but no details of its operation have come to light.

Sanderson's Siding, 1930.

The double track Manchester-Wigan and Bolton line runs from southeast to north-west, bridged by the Manchester Collieries line connecting Sandhole Colliery to the north with the Bridgewater canal to the south. The interchange facilities are extensive, comprising loops and holding sidings, testament to the extent of coal traffic at this location.

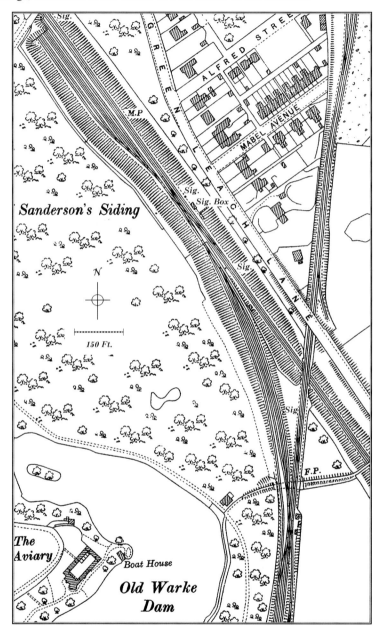

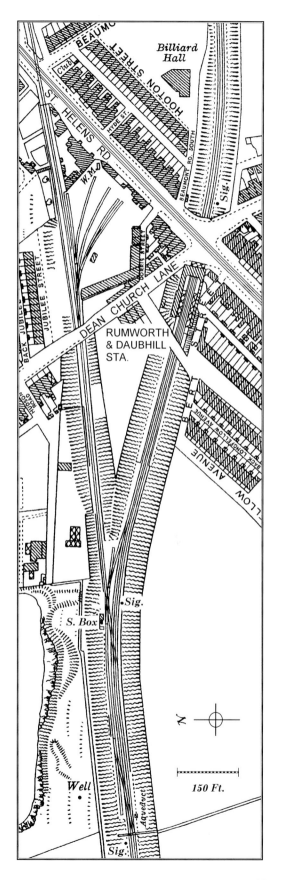

Rumworth & Daubhill, 1930. (right)

The double track deviation line of 1885 is seen running in a cutting to join the Bolton and Leigh formation at Rumworth & Daubhill signal box. The Hulton Collieries coal yard at Rumworth and Daubhill was cramped and quite basic, with no mechanised loading or unloading facilities and beyond it the single track can be seen heading east across St. Helens Rd. on its way to the yard at Sunnyside Mills (Adelaide St.).

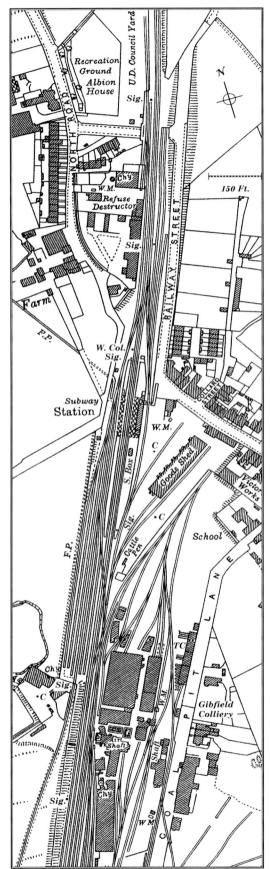

Atherton Bag Lane, c1930.

The close proximity of the yard to the Gibfield Colliery sidings is evident (bottom right). Note also the extensive bank of sidings on the west side of the line, where trains for Hulton Sidings and Bolton were held while waiting for assistance from the banker. The Chequerbent bank began just after the lines crossed the road connecting Railway Street to North Road. The signal box is located in an unusual position on the down platform of the station, but ideally placed to control trains leaving the holding sidings. The Atherton U.D.C. private siding is located to the west of the running lines north of the station.

Plate 25. A view of Bolton Gt. Moor St. station taken from the foot of the ramp at the end of platform 4 on 7th December 1963. The war-time brick-built air raid shelter on platform 1 is visible (left), and the extent to which the overall roof was cut back during the 1930's is evident. Photo, Author.

Plate 26. The water tank on the up (Manchester) side of Bolton Gt. Moor St., also taken on 7th December 1963. The girders in the foreground carry the lines over Crook St., the abutment for the bridge being visible to the right of the brick base of the water tank. Photo, Author.

Chapter 2.

The Engine Sheds At Plodder Lane

EARLY LOCOMOTIVE FACILITIES IN THE BOLTON AREA

The site and nature of locomotive servicing facilities in the Bolton area prior to the construction of the engine sheds at Plodder Lane are a matter of some conjecture, due in part to the indiscriminate use of the term 'Engine House' on early maps and plans. This description was applied not only to a locomotive shed, but also to stationary plant, such as the winding engines for the Daubhill incline and other facilities such as stationary pumping engines, which were often served by rail.

What is known is that the winding engine house on the original formation at Chequerbent had been replaced by a locomotive shed 'for three engines' some time prior to 1867, by which time it was considered by Mr. Ramsbottom, the L&NWR Locomotive Superintendent, to be inadequate for the purpose, being cramped and having no facilities for the washing out of locomotive boilers. As an interim solution a short-lived shed at Leigh was constructed in the 1860's. It is likely that the Chequerbent shed remained in use until the rebuilding of the Bolton and Leigh line in 1885 as discussed above, but no definitive date for its closure has so far emerged.

In Bolton, a shed was provided in the Crook St. area, presumably from early times. The L&NWR locomotive committee minutes refer in 1871 to its removal owing to 'station alterations', obviously a reference to the reconstruction of Great Moor Street station and the expansion of Crook Street yard going on at that time in connection with the new direct line to Manchester, but its precise location is unclear. Early maps, including a survey of the area dated 1870 prepared to illustrate the relationship between existing lines and the new facilities at Great Moor Street, give no direct indication as which, if any, of the rail-accessible buildings in the Crook Street area was used for locomotive purposes, but the engine shed is thought to have been in the building with rail access from two directions, located in the centre of Crook Street yard. This facility, which was

demolished in 1871, had been quite extensive in earlier times, and according to Wishaw had in 1842 been home to two passenger and four goods engines, serviced by a staff of 34 workmen and eight sets of enginemen. A later plan of 1876, which locates an 'Engine House' at the end of the original line and adjacent to the Soho Foundry, is clearly referring to stationary plant, presumably that used to power the newly installed hydraulic system of the Crook St. warehouses and shunting capstans.

Plate 27. An unusual view of bridge 24, immediately to the south of Plodder Lane station, in October 1951. The station buildings are visible in the background, together with the fixed distant signal for the Plodder Lane No. 2 home signal. Bridge 24 carried the line over a road that in earlier times had given access to a sandstone quarry on the down side of the line.

Photo, Harry Jack.

There is no evidence of any locomotive facilities on the Little Hulton line or in the Plodder Lane area prior to the extension of the line from Little Hulton to Bolton in 1874; indeed the Plodder Lane area had no rail connections of any kind until the Little Hulton Extension Railway was built, those works incorporating the construction of the engine shed at Plodder Lane. In contrast to the goods and passenger facilities at Plodder Lane, which remained essentially unchanged from opening to closure, the locomotive facilities were to see many changes during that period, encompassing a period of expansion and improvement into the 1920's, followed by retrenchment and decline until closure in 1954.

Although the expenditure of £9,000 for the new engine shed was not approved until July 1874, the L&NWR had clearly been planning the construction of such facilities for some time. The Farnworth rates books for the period show that the large area of land (5.85 acres or 2.37 hectares) subsequently used for the engine shed and goods yard was first leased to the L&NWR by its then owners, the Trustees of the Cockey Moor Chapel, in 1872, although the land was not purchased by the railway company until 1874, when the L&NWR is listed for the first time as the owner and occupier of 'land and buildings at Fishpool'. Work in the area had begun much sooner than this, however, as the girders for the overbridge at Plodder Lane were cast by Howarth & Cryer of Bolton in 1871 and the Bolton Evening News for 30th. March 1871 reported that the railway contractors. Messrs. Knight and Pilling, were already at work in the area between the workhouse and Plodder Lane. The first year for which rates for the L&NWR were recorded was 1876, the rateable values being listed as: railway £159.0.0, stations

Plodder Lane, c1910

The most obvious change since 1891 is the completion of the track layout into the new shed building. Other changes include the removal of the station crossover and the expansion of the stables located in the entrance road to the goods yard.

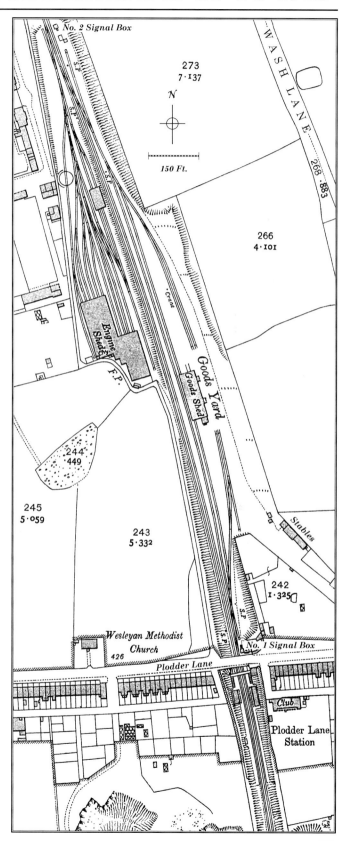

stations £42.10.0, engine shed £76.10.0, resulting in the collection of rates of: railway £5.9.4, stations £4.5.0, engine shed £7.13.0. For comparison, the Lancashire and Yorkshire Railway's establishment in Farnworth was assessed a rateable value of: railway £1263.0.0, stations £180.0.0, reflecting both the relative remoteness of Plodder Lane from the business centre of Farnworth and the more central location of the L&Y station.

The original L&NWR engine shed building at Plodder Lane was designed in the Ramsbottom hipped-roof style to accommodate twelve locomotives. Built on the west side of the running lines, with covered four roads and bay-windowed office accommodation at the rear, the shed was about 60 ft. wide and 120 ft. long, and opened in 1875. It was accessible to pedestrians by a 6 ft. wide footpath that ran from Plodder Lane to Minerva road along the western boundary of the railway property, but was never provided with road access of any kind. The official entrance to the shed was a gate in the wall by the office area. The shed could also be reached from the goods yard by crossing the running lines, and over the years several unofficial entrances came into existence, one being a series of wooden strips nailed to the sleeper fence at the end of Silverdale Road in the northeast corner of the goods yard. The shed was provided with gas lighting, controlled by a set of valves at the entrance to the shed. Each valve controlled a section of lights, and in theory the lights were ignited by pilot light when the valves were opened.

The updated construction plan of 1876 shows the other facilities provided in the form of a 42 ft. turntable and a water tank. Although no indication of the coaling facilities is provided, these would almost certainly have been incorporated beneath the

Plodder Lane, c1929.

A careful examination of the layout in the shed yard shows minor changes when compared with the 1910 map, particularly in the vicinity of the turntable and the key points giving access to the new shed building. The headshunt at the southern end of the goods yard has now been removed, as has the down line signal north of the Plodder Lane bridge, leaving No. 1 signal box with fewer responsibilities.

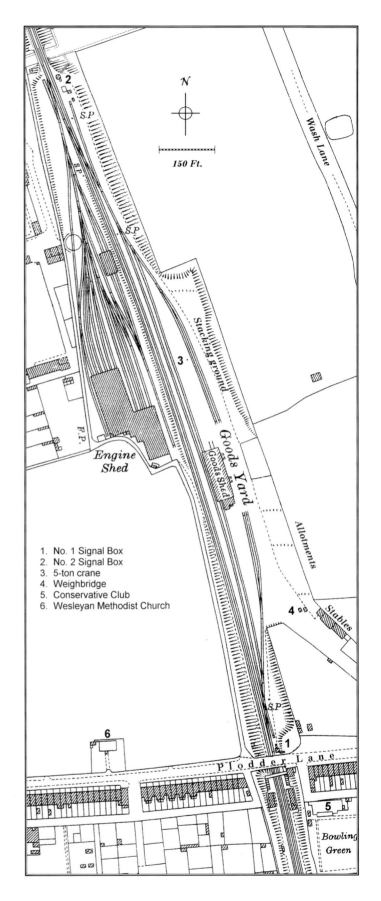

1. No. 1 Signal Box
2. No. 2 Signal Box
3. 5-ton crane
4. Weighbridge
5. Conservative Club
6. Wesleyan Methodist Church

water tank in the standard L&NWR manner. This small shed must soon have proved to be inadequate for the traffic of the district; the closure of Chequerbent shed would have placed an additional strain on the Plodder Lane facility, and in 1890 a considerable enlargement of the latter was put in hand. This comprised a new six-road shed of 79 ft. in width and 166 ft. in length, built in the standard Webb northlight style with 11 roof sections, the first nine from the entrance carrying six smoke ventilators on each section, with five on the rearmost two sections to allow for a sand-drying furnace to be incorporated in the south-west corner.

The new building adjoined the west side of the original four-road shed, but was offset to the north. A road for sand wagons and coal storage was provided outside the western wall of the new shed and the sand-drying furnace was also located here, but the building was otherwise bare of accoutrements as the office accommodation, stores, fitting shop and mess rooms of the old shed were all present at the rear of the old shed building, which was retained intact. To accommodate the new shed, the turntable was moved northwards to the position it would occupy for almost the next 50 years by the footpath leading along the west side of the railway property, and a new, larger, coaling stage/water tank,

59 ft. by 33 ft. in size, was constructed adjacent to the running lines. The latter was unusual among L&NWR coaling stages in that it had a double ramp for coal wagons, running into the stage from both directions, instead of the single ramp favoured elsewhere, but there was no shortage of space at Plodder Lane. The new turntable site was considerably higher than the path, which was hemmed in by high walls on both sides at this location, and the turntable itself was supported by a part-circular stone retaining wall topped by iron railings. A small section of this boundary wall is all that now remains of the railway installations at Plodder Lane.

The Ordnance Survey of 1890 shows the shed at an interim stage in the expansion, with the new building in place and the turntable in its new location, but with the original water tank still present. This would clearly have to be removed to allow the roads to be laid into the new shed. By the 1920's the shed had reached its fullest development. The track plan shown on the 1910 OS map was modified slightly in the 1920's to facilitate access to the turntable and the shed roads, but the basic facilities were unchanged from the 1890 expansion, and it was during the period from 1890 to 1920 that the shed reached its zenith.

Plate 28. The water tank and coaling plant at Plodder Lane, 21st. July 1964. This view, taken across the running lines, also shows No. 2 signal box in the far background. Comparison with earlier photographs shows that the air-raid spotter's hut on the left hand corner of the water tank has either collapsed or been removed. It is not evident in this view.

Photo, Author.

49

Plate 29. Looking north from the Plodder Lane bridge on 18th. September 1955, over a year after the cessation of passenger trains, shows that the goods yard is in use for its intended traffic, and is also being used for the storage of withdrawn coaching stock. On the left the roof of Plodder Lane sheds can be seen, the truncated roof of the original four-road shed adjacent to the footpath leading from Plodder Lane and, to its left, the cut-back roof of the later 6 road shed. The curious vertical structure visible on the left corner of the water tank is the air raid spotter's hut. As was usual in later years, all the signals in this view are in the 'off' position.

Photo, Harry Jack.

Plate 30. The view of Plodder Lane from No. 2 signal box on 21st. July 1964. The signal posts are all devoid of arms, but the hut and goods shed on the left remain unchanged from former times. The exit roads from the shed yard are visible to the right of the running lines, and the entrance to the air-raid shelter can be discerned to the immediate right of the most northerly post in this area.

Photo, Author.

50

By the early 1930's the original four-road shed building was almost 60 years old and showing signs of its age. Prior to 1937 the roof of the old shed was cut back, leaving only a small section at the rear together with the offices, stores, fitting shop and mess room (in that order from the running lines). The stores was fitted with a Dutch door, the lower part of which carried a counter on which oil bottles could be handed in for filling, and to prevent this being open to the elements once the roof was removed a glass walled 'shed' was built to enclose the entrance to the stores. This enclosure also formed the driver's lobby and held a desk; on the wall were roster cases and notice boards. Drivers booked in this lobby, drawing their time cards from the storekeeper and returning them along with repair cards at the end of a shift. The east wall of the old shed was left standing until 1938/9, at which time the newer shed was also substantially altered. At this time, the outer wall of the old shed was removed, and the new shed building was cut back by 60 feet to approximately two-thirds of its original length, leaving only seven of the roof sections intact, and a set of engine inspection pits out in the open in front of the new shed entrance. The cast iron columns that had supported the former entrance to the six-road shed were left in situ for a brief time, but removed for scrap at the start of the war, but the site of the former shed entrance could still be discerned on the ground by the concrete bases for these pillars, which remained until the site was cleared in the 1950's.

The shed was served by the town water supply, but in the early 1930's an attempt was made to reduce the costs involved by the provision of treated water from a large holding tank at Trinity St. station in Bolton. This tank, which was supplied from a well at Bromley Cross, was already in use to supply water to the Trinity St. area and the L&YR sheds at Burnden, and a 9in. diameter pipe was built from the tank to a pump in the cutting of the Bolton to Lostock line, then vertically up the side of the

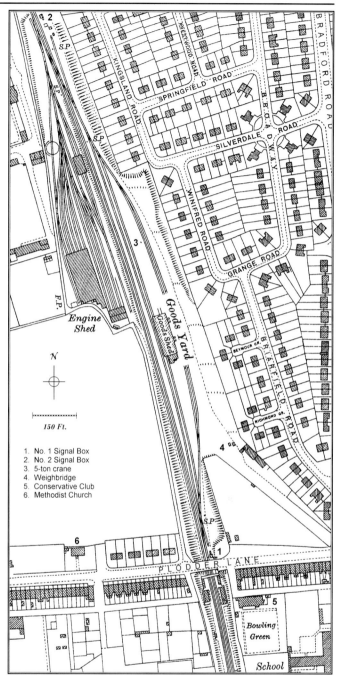

Plodder Lane, c1938.

Although the track layout in the shed yard is unchanged from that of 1929, this map shows that the removal of buildings has begun. The original four-road shed has lost most of its roof, but the outer wall closest to the running lines is still extant. Also noteworthy are the extent of urban development to the east of the goods yard, and the appearance of Marsh Lane School south of the Conservative Club.

Plate 31. This view on 18th. September 1955, a year after closure, shows the shed buildings as seen from the footpath that ran from Plodder Lane. The shed entrance, the wooden gate on the right, gave immediate access to the remains of the 4-road shed building, only the office section of which remained at this time. The newer six-road building, with its rows of smoke ventilators on the roof, is visible to the left. The large chimney on the extreme left identifies the location of the sand-drying furnace in the corner of this building.

Photo, Harry Jack.

Plate 32. This view of the Plodder Lane shed yard in May 1949 shows, from left to right, an almost new 2-6-2T, No.41216, an unidentified 4F 0-6-0, 2-6-2T No. 41212, 4F 0-6-0 No.44356, and an unidentified L&NWR 0-8-0. It also shows the front of the shed roof in good repair, and, on the ground in front of the locomotives, the circular bases for the pillars that supported the shed roof when at its fullest extent. Note the coaching stock stored in the goods yard on the far side of the running lines.

Photo, J.H.Tonge.

cutting to Gt. Moor St. station, and along the line from Gt. Moor St. to Plodder Lane. The new installation was, however, unsuccessful, as the vertical rise between Bolton and Plodder Lane defeated the pumping capacity, and Plodder Lane continued to use town water for the remainder of its existence.

As part of the 1938 LM&SR Engine Turntable Renewal Programme the sum of £3,331 was allocated for replacement of the 42 ft. manual turntable at Plodder Lane by a new vacuum-operated 60 ft. turntable, situated in front of the offices at the end of the old shed site. The track layout was modified slightly in order to allow access to the turntable from two roads, and to provide a through road over the site of the old turntable, but was otherwise unchanged. There is no evidence to support the long-held local belief that this new turntable was intended for the former L&YR sheds on Crescent Road at Burnden in Bolton, but installed at Plodder Lane 'by mistake'. Its installation at Plodder Lane was clearly part of a comprehensive revamping of that shed for the upcoming hostilities. In all likelihood, in the light some knowledge of the characters involved and the rivalry that existed between footplate staff at the two sheds, the story originated and was perpetuated at Crescent Road from feelings of jealousy at a new facility being provided to the 'other place'. Burnden shed did not get a new vacuum-operated turntable until the early 1950's.

The second world war brought only minor changes to the infrastructure at Plodder Lane shed. An air raid shelter was dug into the west side of the shed yard close to Plodder Lane No. 2 signal box, and an aircraft spotterís hut for use during air raids was constructed in an ludicrously exposed position on

Plodder Lane, c1951

The final layout of the shed is shown here. The new 60 ft. turntable is present on the site of the original four-road shed, and the newer six-road shed has been cut back to expose six inspection pits outside the surviving building. The air-rail shelter is shown on the west side of the shed property in a position convenient to No. 2 signal box, but a long way from the shed buildings in an emergency.

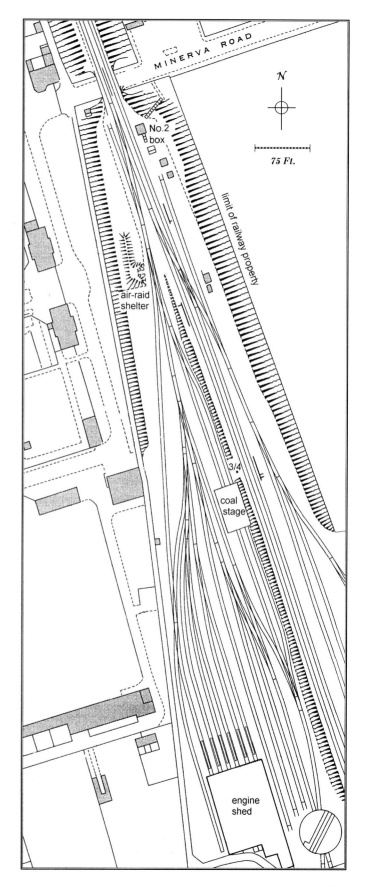

MINERVA ROAD

N

75 Ft.

No.2 box

limit of railway property

air-raid shelter

3/4

coal stage

engine shed

top of the water tank. The immediate post-war years were to see major changes, however, and as passenger and freight traffic declined or were diverted elsewhere, it was soon to become clear that the shed was living on borrowed time.

Plate 33. This view, taken in the Autumn of 1949, shows Plodder Lane sheds as it would be seen from the entrance gate on the footpath from the road. The bay window belongs to the foreman's office, and behind it are the truncated remains of the Ramsbottom 4-road shed building. Just visible beyond this is the new 60 ft. turntable. The cast iron sign in the right foreground warned intending trespassers that their presence was not appreciated: in any event, unofficial visitors rarely got past the foreman's office window.

Photo, Harry Jack.

Plate 34. (Below) After the cessation of passenger trains, Plodder Lane was home to freight locomotives, typified by the collection shown here on 9th. May 1954. From left to right the locomotives visible are 4F 0-6-0 No.44261, L&NWR 0-8-0's Nos.49147 and 49149, 3F 0-6-0T No.47401, 2-6-2T No.84004, and L&NWR 0-8-0's Nos.49203 and 49034. The exception, passenger tank No.84004, was retained at Plodder Lane for several months after the end of normal passenger services in order to work the unadvertised workmen's trains from Bolton to Monton Green.

Photo, A.B.Crompton.

Chapter 3.

The Locomotive History
of
Plodder Lane,
1874-1954.

The often-used division of locomotive histories into the convenient periods prior to the company grouping in 1923, the 'big four' era of 1923 to 1948, and post nationalisation in 1948, has little relevance to the story of Plodder Lane's locomotives. The shed began life under the London and North Western Railway, was stocked with their locomotives, and essentially continued as such almost until closure. Engines came and went, but, as with the shed buildings, the dominant locomotive theme was laid down by the L&NWR and the latter remained remarkably unchanged.

Much of the following information was obtained from the records of the Engine Shed Society, whose members were assiduous at recording events at even the most remote locations.

The earliest allocation list for Plodder Lane that is known is dated November 11th. 1912, at which time it was responsible for 36 locomotives. Plodder Lane was then coded by the L&NWR as shed '34P' (a sub-shed of Patricroft, coded '34'), and was home to the following:

Class B 0-8-0 4-cylinder compound freight engines: 41, 500, 859, 1044, 1091, 1278, 1279, 1283, 2057, 2568 (total 10). These were the most modern engines then at Plodder Lane, the class having been introduced in August 1901. All the above were subsequently rebuilt as class G1 2-cylinder simple expansion engines by the LMSR and seven (Nos. 500, 859, 1044, 1091, 1278, 1279, 2568) were rebuilt again as class G2a. One of these, L&NWR No. 1278, which became LM&SR No. 9381 and BR No. 49381, lasted another 50 years, not being withdrawn from service until November 1962.

18" Goods 0-6-0 engines: 454 and 909 (total 2) were also relatively new engines, built in 1900 and 1897 respectively, but to a design dating from 1880. Although officially designated as goods engines, locomotives of this type, later known as 'cauliflowers', were often used on passenger trains as their 5'2½" diameter driving wheels gave them a useful turn of speed.

0-6-0 Coal Engines: 93, 226, 1291, 1319, 2105, 2426 (total 6). All these locomotives had already seen considerable service in 1912. The oldest, 1291, had been built in April 1873 and even the youngest, 2105, was twenty years old. Nos. 1291, 1319 and 2105 were transferred to the army R.O.D. in 1917 and one of these, 1319, survived until British Railways days, being withdrawn as No. 28271 (allocated 58335 but never renumbered), in December 1948.

DX Goods 0-6-0 engines: 3036, 3055, 3414 (total 3). At fifty one years old, 3414 was the oldest engine at Plodder Lane in 1912, having been built in February 1861. It was withdrawn in August 1913, but 3036, built in August 1864, was to survive until July 1926.

4'6" Class 2-4-2T: 131, 136, 892, 951, 969, 1181, 2246 (total 7). A class designed for local passenger traffic, dating from 1879. Nos. 131 and 136 were built in 1882, the youngest of the class at Plodder Lane being Nos. 951 and 1181 of 1898. The latter locomotive was sold in 1914 to the Cardiff Railway and became their No. 14 *The Earl of Dumfries*. In 1922 it was absorbed by the Great Western Railway and briefly became GWR No. 1327, being withdrawn in May of the same year.

Coal Tank 0-6-2T: 205, 242, 595, 996 (total 4). No. 205, one of the earliest examples of the class, built in 1881, survived until December 1949, when it was withdrawn as BR No.58883.

Special Tank 0-6-0ST: 1453, 3133, 3298, 3373 (total 4). Of these venerable engines, three were already on the duplicate list (numbered in the 3XXX series) by 1912.

The locomotive duties allocated to Plodder Lane were discharged as follows: the 0-8-0 and 0-6-0 locomotives were responsible the coal and goods traffic, heavier and long distance trains being handled by the former, while the latter handled local traffic and trip workings; the local passenger traffic was in charge of the 2-4-2T and 0-6-2T classes; and shunting duties in Crook St. Yard were undertaken by the 0-6-0ST 'Special Tanks'.

Plate 35. A coal tank, built in July 1886 as L&NWR 2878, is seen here as LMS No. 7737. The engine had worked light from the sheds at Plodder Lane to Tyldesley, spent its shift working between there and Kenyon Jn., and is seen here at Roe Green Jn. on its way back to Plodder Lane at 5.15pm, on a day in October 1948. No. 7737 had been at Plodder since at least 1944, but was to remain for only a month after this photograph was taken. It was transferred to Monument Lane sheds in Birmingham when displaced at Plodder Lane by the arrival of the LM&SR 2-6-2T's in November, 1948.   Photo, J.H.Tonge.

Plate. 36. Although there is no record of L&NWR 0-8-0 compound freight engine No.2557 having been allocated to Plodder Lane, it represents a class of engine that was common at the shed, probably from its introduction in 1901. L&NWR 2557 was built at Crewe in August 1902 and is seen prior to 1923 in Plodder Lane shed yard. This is the only photograph known to have been taken at Plodder Lane in L&NWR days, and it has been suggested that it might be dated by checking the local hospital records for a case of removal of someone stuck in a locomotive chimney! The personnel that can be identified in this view are Billy Bridge (on the locomotive chimney) and Bob Hindle (second from the right).

Photo, M.Mitchell.

It is not difficult to speculate on the types of locomotives allocated to Plodder Lane in earlier times. Although no definitive data are available, the range of duties handled by Plodder Lane men and locomotives did not change substantially throughout the lifetime of the shed, so there is little doubt that the nineteenth century allocation would be have been similar in pattern if not in locomotive class to that of 1912, with passenger trains being handled by the Crewe-type 2-4-0T and later the 4'6" 2-4-2T engines, coal and goods traffic in charge of the DX 0-6-0's until the new 0-8-0's became available from the late 1890's onwards, and shunting duties in the hands of the Special 0-6-0ST's.

The continuation of this pattern is evident from a comparison of the allocation of 28 locomotives in October 1917 with the 1912 allocation detailed above. Although none of the locomotives allocated to Plodder Lane in 1912 was still present in 1917, the pattern of locomotive types was unchanged, the allocation now consisting of 28 locomotives comprising:

Class E 2-8-0 compound: 1236 (total, 1), an example of an unusual class, built in 1903 as a class B 0-8-0, rebuilt as a 2-8-0 in 1906 and again as a simple expansion 0-8-0 in 1921.

Class B 0-8-0: 3 examples
Class D 0-8-0: 1 example
Special DX 0-6-0: 2 examples
0-6-0 Coal Engine: 5 examples
18" Goods 0-6-0: 1 example
2-4-2T: 6 examples
18" 0-6-2T: 2 examples
Coal Tank 0-6-2T: 4 examples
0-6-0ST: 3 examples

The next date for which complete allocation data are available is September 1919. By this time, the allocation had fallen to 26, but the pattern of locomotive types was unchanged, consisting of:

Class B 0-8-0: 1224, 1248, 2556 (total 3). Nos. 1224 and 1228 were the newest of the allocation, dating from 1903. Both were in service until December 1962.

Special DX 0-6-0: 3058, 3429 (total, 2). These two locomotives were the oldest then at Plodder Lane, having been built in July 1867 and June 1869, respectively.

Coal Engine 0-6-0: 3170, 3286, 3354, 3384, 3488 (total, 5).

4'6" Class 2-4-2T: 284, 298, 889, 2501, 2506 (total 5). Nos. 284 and 889 were subsequently sold to the Wirral Railway, in 1921 and 1920 respectively, and so came to the LM&SR from WR rather than L&NWR ownership.

5'6" Class 2-4-2T: 1018, 1153, 2137, 2141 (total 4)
18" Class 0-6-2T: 586, 973 (total, 2)
Coal Tank Class 0-6-2T: 2485 (total,1)
Special Tank 0-6-0ST: 3073, 3263, 3337, 3597 (total, 4)

The average age of the Plodder Lane allocation at this time was almost 33 years.

During the 1920's the number of 18" Class 0-6-2T's allocated to Plodder Lane increased as they replaced the older 2-4-2 tank locomotives. LMSR Nos. 6874, 6875, 6877 and 6879 of the former class are known to have been among the Plodder Lane allocation during this period, although it is believed that the series 6874-6880 was at Plodder Lane. Their stay was not prolonged, however, for during the early 1930's the 18" tanks were gradually replaced by coal tanks, the latter with their smaller driving wheels perhaps being considered more suitable for work over the heavily graded lines served by Plodder Lane engines, and at least four of the latter engines (7590, 7623, 7677 and 7795) were among the Plodder Lane allocation in July 1933.

Grouping of the railways in 1923 also saw the gradual introduction of LMS standard types to Plodder Lane for freight and shunting work, as the MR-derived 0-6-0 designs began to replace the older LNWR 0-6-0 tender and tank locomotives. This is evident from data collected during a visit to the shed on July 12th., 1933 when 13 locomotives were present, Nos. 4066, 4398, 6876, 6878, 6883, 7590, 7623, 7672, 7677, 7795, 7808, 16471, and 16472, with seven others listed on the shed board as out working, viz. nos. 4342, 4357, 4358, 4374, 4494, 9009, and 16473. Of these, 4066, 4342, 4357,

4358, 4374, 4398 and 4494 represented the MR-derived 0-6-0 tender engines, and 16471-16473 the standard 0-6-0 shunting tank design. The passenger traffic was, however, still exclusively in the hands of ex. L&NWR engines in the form of the 0-6-2 coal tanks.

The locomotive situation at Plodder Lane remained remarkably constant throughout the rest of the 1930's. On Sunday March 1st. 1936, 29 locomotives were present at the shed, this total probably representing most if not all of the allocation. Twenty seven of these carried the new '10D' shedplates for Plodder Lane that had been introduced in 1935. The list of locomotives present on that date is:

Class D 0-8-0: 9009 (total, 1).

Class G 0-8-0: 9070, 9127, 9147 (total, 3).

Class 4F 0-6-0: 4059, 4358, 4374, 4379, 4398, 4494 (total, 6).

Coal tank 0-6-2T: 7703, 7715, 7722, 7727, 7756, 7769, 7795, 7806, 7808, 27580, 27586, 27590, 27602, 27621, 27623, 27645 (total, 16).

Class 3F 0-6-0T: 7388, 7389, 7390 (total, 3).

The oldest locomotive then at the shed was coal tank 27590, built in 1881; the average age of the Plodder Lane coal tanks was no less than 51½ years. The next year saw little change in the range of locomotives present, but a reduction in the numbers, perhaps indicative of a decline in traffic. The locomotives present on February 21st. 1937, also a Sunday, were:

L&NWR 0-8-0: 3 examples, including 9009

Class 4F 0-6-0: 4 examples

L&YR 0-6-0: 12394

Coal Tank 0-6-2T: eleven examples, including 27603 and 27605

Class 3F 0-6-0T: 2 examples

Wartime allocation data is scarce, but it is known that a 19" goods engine, 8858, was allocated to Plodder Lane during the 1942/43 period. It was little

Plate 37. Former L&NWR 0-8-0, now LMS No. 9009, was a long-time resident at Plodder Lane. It is seen here, still carrying its yellow LM&SR number, in the shed yard in the Autumn of 1949, and had been at Plodder Lane on and off since at least 1935. During its time at Plodder Lane this engine visited Crewe works at least twice, for it was rebuilt from class D to class G1 in July 1937, and again to class G2a in June 1940, one of the last engines of its type to be dealt with in this way. Photo, Harry Jack.

used, spending much of its time in store at the end of No. 4 road. It was only fired when no other locomotive was available, and working on it was looked on with horror by the footplate staff. By October of 1944 the allocation was reduced even further, but Plodder Lane had received an allocation of two former L&YR 2-4-2T's. As there are no 0-8-0 freight engines listed the allocation data for this date are thought to be incomplete, consisting of:

Class 4F 0-6-0: 4119, 4341, 4352, 4356, 4358, 4379, 4386 (total 7)

Coal tank 0-6-2T: 7722, 7737, 7756, 7758, 7761, 7769, 27590 (total 7)

L&YR 2-4-2T: 10643, 10644 (total 2)

Class 3F 0-6-0T: 7401

On August 26th. 1945, (a Sunday), 19 locomotives were 'on shed', comprising:

L&NWR 0-8-0: 9147, 9378

Class 4F 0-6-0: 4119, 4341, 4352, 4356, 4358, 4379, 4386

5'6" 2-4-2T: 6722 (of Sutton Oak)

Coal tank 0-6-2T: 7722, 7737, 7756, 7761, 7769, 27590

L&YR 2-4-2T: 10643, 10644

Class 3F 0-6-0T: 7401

It is interesting to compare this list with the official allocation for November 1945, given below:

L&NWR 0-8-0: 9147, 9378 (total 2).

Class 4F 0-6-0: 4119, 4341, 4352, 4356, 4358, 4379, 4386 (total 6)

Coal tank 0-6-2T: 7682, 7722, 7737, 7756, 7761, 7769 (total 6).

L&YR 2-4-2T: 10643, 10644 (total 2).

Class 3F 0-6-0T: 7401 (total 1).

The comparison illustrates well the 'local' nature of Plodder Lane as a locomotive shed: the engines present on a Sunday, when few trains were worked, were essentially all Plodder Lane allocations, with only one obvious visitor and few, if any, engines away from home.

The allocation of coal tanks was dramatically reduced from that of pre-war years, but the acquisition of the L&YR 2-4-2 tanks did, at least on paper, somewhat alleviate the loss of some of Plodder Lane's favourite engines. During the next few years Plodder Lane was to become a collecting site for many of the remaining coal tanks. In March, 1946 No. 7761 was withdrawn, to be replaced by 7789, and in January 1947, No. 7722 was replaced by 7823 and 27619. In June of that year, 7682 and 7683 were both withdrawn and the L&Y 2-4-2 tanks transferred to Barrow, but the losses were made good by the transfer of coal tanks 7720, 7799, 7802 and 27586 to Plodder Lane. In September 1947 the latter engine was transferred to Bletchley, leaving Plodder Lane with 8 coal tanks on nationalisation of the railways on January 1st. 1948, Nos. 7720, 7737, 7756, 7769, 7789, 7799, 7802, and 27619. Of these, No. 7799 was later to become better known when reborn in preservation as L&NWR No. 1054.

In March 1948 No. 7769 was withdrawn, and replaced by 27627 from Rhyl, and in June, 27619 was transferred from Plodder Lane to Edge Hill, being replaced by 7752 from Tredegar. In August of that year 7756 was withdrawn. The replacement was not another coal tank however, but a new locomotive, 2-6-2T No. 41215, fresh from Crewe Works and on loan to Plodder Lane for trials. These were evidently successful, thus heralding the end of the coal tank era at Plodder Lane, however, for in November 1948, 41215 was joined by 41210-41214, 41216 and 41217, and the remaining coal tanks were transferred away.

However, this was not quite the end of the coal tanks at Plodder Lane, for in early 1950, 2-6-2T 41210 was transferred to Rhyl for the summer seasonal traffic and replaced temporarily by coal tank 58897 from Edge Hill. The latter stayed only a short while before it was transferred again, this time to Bletchley and L&YR 2-4-2T 50644 came back from Barrow as its replacement. Thus ended the long association of coal tanks with Plodder Lane. They had worked the passenger services from Bolton Great Moor Street successfully for many years, and were also known to have been used on freight trains in an emergency. It is tribute to their efficiency in working the passenger trains on the difficult routes out of Bolton that they were only

Plate 38. LM&SR-designed 2-6-2T No.41212 shows a relatively clean face in its BR livery at Plodder Lane on 22nd. April 1949. The motor gear for push-and-pull working is evident on the side of the smokebox, and the engine is blowing off steam, and so presumably about to leave the shed to work a local passenger train. The passenger tanks at Plodder Lane were normally stabled facing Bolton, as this one is, so that they could work bunker-first down the Chequerbent incline. Photo, Harry Jack.

Plate 39. The fact that most of the Plodder Lane cleaning staff were out on the road as firemen is evident from the state of LM&SR 2-6-2T No.41210, seen here at Roe Green Jn. only a short time after its arrival at Plodder Lane as a new engine from Crewe works in November, 1948. The locomotive is reversing at Roe Green Jn. during a trip as light engine from Tyldesley to Plodder Lane.

Photo, J.H.Tonge.

replaced when a modern design became available some 65 years after the coal tanks were first built.

Towards the end of the coal tank era, a visit to the shed on August 15th. 1948 found the following present:

L&NWR 0-8-0: 9147, 9224, 9257, 9315, 9378, 49065, 49310.

Class 4F 0-6-0: 4119, 4356, 4379.

Coal Tank 0-6-2T: 7720, 7737, 7752, 7789, 7799, 7802.

Class 3F 0-6-0T: 7401.

While just over one year later, on August 28th. 1949, the following engines were present, a collection devoid of a coal tank representative for the first time in many years:

L&NWR 0-8-0: 9009, 49065, 49075, 49101, 49147, 49257, 49315, 49378.

Class 4F 0-6-0: 44119, 44356.

2MT 2-6-2T: 41210, 41211, 41212, 41213, 41214, 41215, 41217.

Class 3F 0-6-0T: 47401.

In mid-1950 the official allocation reflected a reduced need for heavy goods power, and consisted of:

L&NWR 0-8-0: 49101, 49147, 49315. (total 3)

Class 4F 0-6-0: 44237, 44261, 44356, 44384, 44454, 44473. (total 6)

Class 2MT 2-6-2T: 41211, 41212, 41213, 41214, 41215, 41216, 41217. (total 7)

L&YR 2-4-2T: 50644. (total 1)

Class 3F 0-6-0T: 47401 (total 1)

Replacement motive power to allow for scheduled repairs of Plodder Lane engines, either at home if the job was small, or at Springs Branch for larger jobs for which Plodder Lane was not equipped, was supplied by Springs Branch shed in Wigan. This resulted in some ancient machines, unwanted by the larger shed, finding their way to Plodder Lane. Examples of locomotive types known to have been sent from Springs Branch to Plodder Lane in this role during the 1940's include L&YR 0-6-0's of both Barton-Wright and Aspinall design, and L&NWR 'cauliflower' 0-6-0's. A frequent but unpopular visitor was 'cauliflower' 8585, looked on with

horror by Plodder Lane men as it still had wooden brake blocks on the tender. These contained deep holes filled with resin, intended to melt and become sticky during braking, and working tender-first down Chequerbent incline produced clouds of resin-charged wood smoke that choked the footplate crew. L&NWR 2P 2-4-2T's were also supplied on occasion, together with L&NWR 19" goods 4-6-0's, one of the last survivors of which, no. 8824, was noted in Plodder Lane shed yard in this capacity in 1944. On one occasion a set of men had an engine failure at Wigan and were given 'Claughton' 4-6-0 6004 to work back to Plodder Lane, but this was soon reclaimed by the parent shed.

Unlike that of the coal tanks the reign of the LM&SR-designed 2-6-2 tanks at Plodder Lane was to be short lived, and, for some engines, intermittent. No. 41217 was sent to Barrow to work the Coniston branch in September 1951, and L&Y 2-4-2T 50643, a previous occupant of Plodder Lane, came back in its place. The Rhyl engine, 41210, came back to Plodder Lane in November of 1951, only to be replaced at the North Wales shed between June and November 1952 by 41211 from Plodder Lane. In the meantime, the L&Y 2-4-2 tanks 50643 and 50644 had been transferred to Preston in June 1952 and in February 1953, 41211 was transferred to Rugby, only to return to Plodder Lane in June of the same year.

In July 1953 Plodder Lane was to receive its final passenger train engines in the form of BR standard design 2-6-2 tanks 84000-84004 sent new to the shed, and the earlier 2-6-2 tanks of the 4121X series were transferred elsewhere. It was indeed remarkable for a relatively obscure shed such as Plodder Lane to receive a significant number of new locomotives on its allocation, especially when it had made do for so long with such venerable machines as the coal tanks, but in the light of locomotive policy of the era, which saw the construction of almost 1000 new locomotives of BR standard design, it was not a unique event. Similar replacements occurred, for example, on the former Cambrian system, where the LMS and BR 2-6-0

Plate 40. This view on 23rd. July. 1953, was taken during the changeover of passenger motive power at Plodder Lane from the LM&SR-designed 2-6-2T's to the later BR version. Both types are visible, left to right an unidentified LM&SR version, BR No.84001, LM&SR No.41214, LM&SR No.41210, and BR No.84002.

Photo, C.B.Golding.

Plate 41. A visitor to Plodder Lane, LM&SR 2-6-2T No.40003 from Springs Branch shed, is seen at the former location on 17th. May 1953. This locomotive was facing the wrong way to work down the Chequerbent incline, and if being returned to its home shed by that route would have to be turned prior to the journey. The fact that it was stabled in this direction at Plodder Lane suggests that a return trip via Roe Green Jn. and Tyldesley was planned. The 4F 0-6-0 in the background, Plodder Lane's No.44384, was under no such restriction.

Photo, C.B.Golding.

tender engines came to almost monopolise train services in the 1950's

Freight traffic at Plodder Lane, meanwhile, was still handled by class 4F 0-6-0 and ex L&NWR 0-8-0 engines, and the latter were known to have also been occasionally employed on passenger trains, an example being the 07.25 to Manchester on 11th. March 1954, handled by 49034. Several of these engines were still at Plodder Lane at the beginning of 1954, when the allocation of 18 locomotives was composed of:

L&NWR 0-8-0: 49034, 49147, 49149, 49203, 49315. (total 5)

Class 4F 0-6-0: 44237, 44261, 44356, 44384, 44473. (total 5)

LMS 2MT 2-6-2T: 41210, 41214. (total 2)

BR 2MT 2-6-2T: 84000, 84001, 84002, 84003, 84004. (total 5)

Class 3F 0-6-0T: 47401 (total 1)

Perhaps not surprisingly, a visit on 21st. March 1954 (again a Sunday), found all the above locomotives, with the exception of 41210 and 44261, at home. During the early 1950's, however, the presence of other foreign locomotives, usually from Patricroft, under repair at Plodder Lane was also noted, examples including Class 2P 4-4-0's,

Class 5 4-6-0's, and even a 'Jubilee' 4-6-0. In May 1954, just after the local passenger services had ceased, a visit to Plodder Lane identified the presence of the following engines, again almost entirely a 'home team', but with the now noticeable absence of all but one of the passenger tanks:

L&NWR 0-8-0: 49034, 49147, 49149, 49203, 49306.

Class 4F 0-6-0: 44237, 44261, 44356, 44384, 44473.

2MT 2-6-2T: 84004.

Class 3F 0-6-0T: 47401.

On withdrawal of local passenger services in March 1954 the 2-6-2 tank engines had all been transferred elsewhere, with the exception of 84004 that remained at Plodder Lane to work the twice daily unadvertised workmen's trains between Great Moor Street and Monton Green. No. 84004 was later replaced on these services by 2-6-2T No.41287, sent from Patricroft for the purpose. When Plodder Lane engine shed finally closed in November of that year, the latter engine was transferred along with the remaining freight and shunting engines, bringing to an end 78 years of steam locomotive presence at Plodder Lane.

Plate 42. L&NWR 0-8-0 No.49034, a local engine, is on the wagon road outside the six-road shed on 23rd. May 1954. This road was used for the storage of sand and coal wagons, and ran between the shed wall and the outer wall of the property, the latter visible to the right of the locomotive. This was the wall over which many of the photographs of engines in the Plodder Lane shed wall were taken: it was not so high on the footpath side! The flat-topped section of the wall visible to the right of the locomotive's smokebox was rebuilt after that part of the wall collapsed in the early 1940's, and proved a boon to local photographers. It was difficult to balance a camera on the earlier gable-topped wall.

Photo, C.B.Golding.

Chapter 4.

Workings from Plodder Lane.

Plate 43 A nine-coach excursion train, the 13.18 for Llandudno, leaving Bolton behind Class 5 4-6-0 No.45382 on Saturday 29th June 1957. The slow progress of this train down the ramp from the passenger station is watched by a group of shunters standing by the water tower at the entrance to Crook St. yard. The Hick, Hargreaves engineering works (Soho Iron Works) are located behind the train, with their sidings visible above the locomotive.

Photo. E.F.Bentley collection.

FREIGHT WORKINGS, 1874-1922.

Little direct information has emerged on the working of freight trains from Plodder Lane in the earliest days, but the working timetables of the period make it clear that such traffic was intensive in extent and varied in nature. Not all freight workings on the L&NWR's Bolton area lines would have been operated by Plodder Lane, but the freight timetables for the Bolton - Roe Green Junction line in 1885, outlined in Tables 1 and 2, suggest an early pattern of possible workings from Plodder Lane; unfortunately, light engine movements were not shown in the L&NWR working timetables of that period.

	WEEKDAYS								SUNDAYS	
	Mineral	Mineral	Goods	Goods MO	Fast Goods	Mineral	Goods	Fast Goods	Mineral	Mineral
Bolton	00.30	02.10	06.15	09.35	15.13	15.50	16.30	22.00	00.30	02.10
Lever St.			06.40		15.20	16.05	16.40			
Plodder Lane			06.47	09.45	15.25	16.25	17.05			
Little Hulton Junction Arr.	00.45	02.20		09.55	X	16.30	17.10		00.45	02.20
Dep.	01.00	02.35			X	16.45	17.35		01.00	02.35
Walkden Sidings				10.05						
Roe Green Junction				10.12	15.40	16.55	17.45	22.25	01.15	02.50
Sanderson's Siding					15.45	17.00				
Ordsall Lane	02.18	05.10		11.12					02.18	05.10
Notes				A			B	C		

Table 1. Extract from the L&NWR Working Timetable, 1885 (Goods and Mineral services only), Up Line

Passing times shown in italics
A: return working of the 07.40 fast goods from Manchester.
B: to Kenyon, returns at 02.00.
C: to Leeds
X: stops as required

There are several notable features about this timetable. A service of mineral and goods trains is provided on Sunday (no Sunday passenger service was ever provided on this line), but Highfield Sidings were not operating at this time. Sanderson's Siding and Lever St. were served only in the up direction. Most of the traffic was to and from Ordsall Lane in Manchester, and could have been worked by either Plodder Lane or Patricroft locomotives. A daily (Sundays excepted) fast goods train ran from Bolton to Leeds, but in the return direction this ran only on Sundays, suggesting a train of empty vans being returned for the following week's services. One might speculate as to the traffic carried to Leeds, but finished cotton goods must surely have played a considerable part, as over 20,000 workers were employed by the textile industry in Bolton at that time. Legend at Plodder Lane, where these trains were still remembered in the 1940's even though they ceased operation during the first world war, maintained that they were worked by 'Jumbo' 2-4-0's.

The L&NWR freight service over the new line to Manchester was well established by 1885. A survey

Table 2. Extract from the L&NW Working Timetable, (Goods and Mineral services only), Down Line.

WEEKDAYS

	Mineral	Mineral	Goods	Goods	Goods MO	Mineral SX	Mineral	Mineral
Ordsall Lane	00.15	02.45	03.50		07.40			22.40
Sanderson's Siding								
Roe Green Junction	*01.03*	*03.25*			*07.57*	*21.34*	*23.08*	*23.18*
Walkden Sidings					08.05			
Little Hulton Junction Arr.	01.15		X		08.10	21.45	23.20	
Dep.	01.25		X		08.20	22.00	23.30	
Plodder Lane	X		X	07.25	08.30	22.10	23.45	
Lever St								
Bolton	01.35	03.50	04.20	07.32	08.35	22.20	23.55	23.45
Notes			A				B	

SUNDAYS

	Mineral	Mineral	Goods	Fast Goods	Mineral
Ordsall Lane	00.15	02.45			
Sanderson's Siding					
Roe Green Junction	*01.03*	*03.25*	*03.45*	*05.10*	*05.40*
Walkden Sidings					05.55
Little Hulton Junction Arr.	01.15		X	05.25	06.00
Dep.	01.25		X	05.35	06.10
Plodder Lane	X		X	05.45	06.20
Lever St					
Bolton	01.35	03.50	04.15	05.55	06.25
Notes	C		D	E	

Passing times shown in italics
A: From Kenyon, depart 02.00
B: From Atherton & Tyldesley Colliery Co. Siding, depart 22.30
C: Returns at 02.10
D: From Worsley, depart 03.40
E: From Leeds, depart 22.40
X: Stops as required

of railway rates and charges, prepared for the Corporation of Bolton by J.W. Gray and published by them in 1887, records rates from Bolton for traffic to Manchester Liverpool Road, London Road, Longsight and Weaste stations. For longer distance traffic, rates by both L&NWR and L&YR routes were comparable in the majority of cases, but the L&NWR line was favoured at that time for traffic destined for London, Stockport (and stations south) and Wigan.

By the turn of the century Plodder Lane shed employed almost 200 men, most of whom would be engaged on freight duties. To put things in context, the L&YR engine shed at Newton Heath, one of the largest in the Manchester area, employed a staff of around 1000 at this time, but the Plodder Lane contributions to train movement in southern Lancashire were by no means insignificant. Both Bolton (No. 32) and Plodder Lane good shed (No. 209) were numbered among only 174 sites on the L&NWR connected to the national telephone service by 1900 (neither Bletchley nor Crewe were included at this time, and Carlisle had only one number for all its facilities!).

The L&NWR working time tables of 1904 and 1906 shed further light on the freight services of that period. The July 1904 timetable records in its general notes the method for working colliery traffic from the Hulton colliery lines that joined the L&NWR in the centre of Chequerbent bank. These trains did not run to a fixed schedule, but a "suitable time" was arranged between the L&NWR inspector at Chequerbent (unusually specified by name, Inspector Winstanley) and the colliery company, whereupon an engine and van were sent to Chequerbent Box for removal of the loaded traffic. The van was detached on the Chequerbent station side of the crossing on the down main line (towards Atherton), with hand brake applied, and the engine then moved forward to stand a few wagon lengths on the Atherton side of the crossing, also on the down main line. A second engine was used to draw wagons from the colliery siding on to the up main line, then placing them via the crossing directly against the L&NWR train engine, whereupon the brakes were pinned down to secure the wagons on the falling gradient. As each run of wagons was removed from the colliery line, the L&NWR engine moved forward until all the wagons were attached, at which time the brake van was dropped down onto the train, which was limited to 24 wagons in the down direction. The engine moving the rakes of loaded wagons out of the colliery siding had by far the hardest work, as each trip involved working up the incline towards Chequerbent before dropping the wagons back down onto the train engine.

All trains on the Chequerbent incline were subject to special restrictions: in July 1904 it was noted for goods trains in the down direction that "all down goods, etc., trains must come to a stand at Chequerbent station box to pick up a bank rider, and must again come to a stand at the bank head to allow the bank rider to alight. Trains must not pass on to the incline until sufficient number of breaks have been applied". This instruction presumably refers to the bank rider as one whose duties were to pin down wagon brakes between Chequerbent box and the start of the incline beyond the station. It does not infer that the bank rider actually travelled with the train on the incline, but the use of the name is surely a continuation from the days when a bank rider was literally that, riding the wagons while they were hauled or lowered by rope from the stationary engine.

The appendix to the July 1906 working timetable contains notes on the provision of banking engines that include their use for goods and mineral trains between Monton Green and Plodder Lane, and also

Plate 44. As late as 7th. December 1963, the booking office on the ground level at Bolton Gt. Moor St. station looked like it was ready to reopen for business. The curved, wooden-panelled front was a characteristic feature. The gas lamp, the bench on the far right and the overall clean appearance belie the fact that regular passenger trains had ceased to run almost ten years earlier.

Photo, Author.

throughout between Worsley and Bolton. The details of the 1906 timetable show a slightly different pattern of freight services from those operating in 1885. Sunday service was much reduced, but overall the service was expanded, with trains from the Manchester direction now originating at Liverpool Road Goods and Patricroft, and Highfield Sidings were now in operation. Walkden Sidings showed little activity, but a new entry was the fascinatingly named 'pig train', running daily from Ordsall Lane to Bolton. Some light engine movements from Plodder Lane were now included, a daily service to Liverpool (Edge Hill) was now present, and the through Leeds service still ran as before. The 1906 timetable, summarised in Tables 3 and 4, amply illustrates the way in which the L&NWR freight services from Bolton, some with engines from Plodder Lane, extended over much of the south Lancashire area at that time.

Plate 45. An ex L.M.S. 4F, stood on Crook St. bridge, is photographed by the signalman at Bolton No.1 cabin, Mr Green, in early 1942 prior to shunting Dawes St. coal drops.

The signalman was a member of Bolton Camera Club, one of who's members owned Morris' camera shop and hence the availability of film which was in short supply during the war years.

As viewed, on the left is driver George Hampson, Jimmy Jones, who kindly supplied the photo, in the middle and Jack Edge, shunter, on the right.

Plate 46. On 26th. February 1959, L&NWR 0-8-0 No.49199, of Patricroft shed, is seen climbing the gradient between Roe Green Jn. and Walkden with a train of coal from Newton or Wheatsheaf collieries, destined for the coal preparation plant at Mosley Common by way of Walkden exchange sidings. The precise location is the footpath that crossed the line between Roe Green Jn. and the East Lancashire road bridge.

Photo, G.Hayes.

Table 3. Extract from the L&NWR Working Timetable, July 1906 (Goods and Mineral services only), Up Line										
	WEEKDAYS									
	Goods MX	Mineral	Goods	Goods MX	Mineral	Goods	Mineral	Mineral	Mineral	Mineral SO
Bolton	00.01	02.30	06.15	08.55		12.45			15.30	
Lever St.	*00.04*	*02.33*	*06.18*	*09.00*		*12.48*			*15.34*	
Plodder Lane	<u>00.15</u>	02.50	06.25	<u>09.05</u>	11.40	<u>12.52</u>			16.00	
Little Hulton Junction Arr.		<u>03.00</u>							16.05	
Dep.							13.40	15.20	16.30	16.25
Walkden Sidings									16.40	16.45
Roe Green Junction										
Notes			A		B	C	D	E		F

	WEEKDAYS				**SUN**
	Goods TuO	Fast Goods	Goods	Mineral	Mineral
Bolton	16.30	21.05	22.10	23.00	03.00
Lever St.	*16.33*	*21.08*	*22.13*	*23.03*	*03.03*
Plodder Lane			<u>22.15</u>		<u>03.10</u>
Little Hulton Junction Arr.	16.45			23.10	
Dep.				23.25	
Walkden Sidings					
Roe Green Junction		*21.25*		*23.33*	
Notes		G	H	I	

Passing times shown in italics
A: departs Plodder Lane at 07.00 to Highfield Sidings, arrive 07.04
B: from Plodder Lane to Highfield Sidings, arrive 11.45
C: to Patricroft arrive 14.05
D: to Patricroft arrive 15.40
E: shunts at Lever St. from 15.34 to 15.40. Calls at Highfield Sidings as required. To Kenyon.
F: to Sanderson's Siding arrive 16.57
G: to Cleckheaton on weekdays, runs to Copley Hill on Saturdays
H: From Atherton depart 20.35
I: to Longsight, Manchester

Plate 47. Ivatt 2-6-2T No.41213 is seen at Kenyon Junction on 3rd. May 1949 with a Bolton Gt. Moor St. push-pull service. That this engine is one of the push-pull variety is acertained by the apparatus fitted to the smoke box.

Photo, W.D.Cooper.

Table 4. Extract from the L&NWR Working Timetable, July 1906 (Goods and Mineral services only), Down Line

	WEEKDAYS											
	Express Goods	Mineral	Express Goods	L.E.	Mineral	Mineral MO	Goods	L.E.	Empties	Mineral Empties	Mineral	Pig Train
Roe Green Junction	02.02X		04.52X		06.45	07.10	07.09					13.10
Walkden Sidings					X							
Little Hulton Junction Arr.			X		06.55	07.30	07.32					X
Dep.		03.20			07.00							
Plodder Lane	02.30	03.40	X	06.50				09.20	11.15	12.20	13.20	
Lever St	02.35	03.47	05.07		07.10				11.28			13.27
Bolton	02.40	03.50	05.10	06.57	07.15	07.45		09.26	11.33			13.30
Notes	A		B		C	D	E		F	G	H	I

Passing times shown in italics
A: from Ordsall Lane, depart 01.45
B: from Liverpool Road Goods, depart 03.55
C: Engine and van depart Patricroft 06.00 to Sanderson's Siding, thence depart with train at 06.35 to Bolton
D: from Patricroft depart 06.30
E: from Patricroft depart 07.00
F: to Edge Hill, Liverpool
G: from Highfield Sidings depart 12.15
H: From Highfield Sidings depart 13.15
I: from Ordsall Lane depart 12.50
X: stops as required

L&NWR Working Timetable, July 1906 (Goods and Mineral services only), Down Line (continued)

	WEEKDAYS											
	Goods SO	Mineral	Mineral TuSX	Mineral TuO	Empties	Mineral	Goods	Goods	Mineral	Goods	Goods	ECS
Roe Green Junction			15.08	15.08		17.07			18.40	19.20	21.32	
Walkden Sidings						17.15						
Little Hulton Junction Arr.			15.23	15.23		17.25			19.05	19.40	21 55	
Dep.			15.35	15.35		17.30					22 55	
Plodder Lane	15.05	15.00	15.40	15.40	16.00		18.25	19.00	19.10			
Lever St	15.08	15.05		15.45	16.05		18.30	19.07	19.42		22.36	
Bolton	15.12	15.30		15.50	16.10		18.32	19.10	19.45		22.40	23.40
Notes		J			K	L			M	N	O	P

Passing times shown in italics
J: shunts Lever Street yard from 15.05 to 15.25. To West Leigh
K: to Edge Hill, Liverpool
L: from Sandersonís Siding depart 17.05
M: shunts at Plodder Lane from 19.10 to 19.35.
From Manchester Ship Canal Co.'s. Siding, depart 17.40
N: from Patricroft depart 19.10
O: from Patricroft depart 21.15
P: empty passenger stock from Patricroft, depart 23.20
Q: from Copley Hill, Leeds, depart 01.30

	SUNDAYS
	Fast Goods
Roe Green Junction	05.25
Plodder Lane	05.43
Lever Street	05.48
Bolton	05.53
Notes	Q

Freight services on the Bolton and Kenyon line during this period were intense. The July 1904 working timetable shows that the line was open every day of the week, with a passenger service on Sunday and goods and mineral services suspended only for a brief period on Sundays. The down line timetable of goods and mineral trains for that period shows 32 paths for such trains on the Bolton and Kenyon line, 8 of which were conditional (ran as required). Of the total, 7 were mineral (presumably coal) trains from Hulton Sidings to destinations such as Garston (Liverpool) (2), Oldham (1), Warrington (1), and Ordsall Lane (Salford) (3), including one to the latter destination specified as 'Loco. Coal'. The longer distance daily goods trains ran from Bolton to Springs Branch (Wigan), Liverpool, Preston (via Atherton), and Warrington, in addition to which mineral trains ran from Bolton to Edge Hill (Liverpool), Ordsall Lane, Wigan, and Warrington. Superimposed on this traffic were shorter goods and mineral trains from Bolton to Little Hulton Junction, Atherton, and Leigh, and the many trip workings to serve sidings in the area, in addition to special workings not shown in the timetable. Around the turn of the century loaded coal specials from Hulton Sidings to Garston docks in Liverpool were a regular occurrence.

Workings in the up direction from the Kenyon line into Bolton largely mirrored those of the down trains, the first arrival of the week in Bolton being the 05.55 goods from Tyldesley, due at 06.45 on a Monday morning, and the last arrival, the 22.25 express goods from Edge Hill, due at 01.15 on Sunday mornings. Plodder Lane locomotives in the form of the L&NWR compound 0-8-0 freight engines were known to have worked through to Garston with coal shipments during this period, which ran via Howe Bridge West Junction and St. Helens, unlike the trains to Edge Hill that joined the Liverpool route at Kenyon Junction.

On the eve of the railway grouping, in October 1922, the local freight workings were little changed from those of 1904/1906, and the majority of long distance services were intact, but the through trains to Leeds no longer ran, and the service to Liverpool was reduced from that of the pre-war years. One consequence of this was a complete absence of freight working on Sundays, so that Crook Street yard was now closed between Saturday evening and Monday morning.

Plate 48. The station at Atherleigh in February 1956. This station, situated on the border of Atherton and Leigh, was opened as recently as 14th October 1935, but had a short working life, closing on 27th. March. 1954. It is thought, however, that the station was used by specials for rugby league games for several years thereafter, as was the nearby Westleigh station.

Photo, G.J.Hardy.

SHUNTING AND TRIP WORKINGS

The shunting and trip workings from Plodder Lane formed a substantial part of the shed's duties, but, with the exception of trips on the Deansgate Branch, did not appear in the early working timetables. The line to Deansgate was operated as set out below in July 1904, with a note in the timetable that "Four competent men from the Goods Department will accompany the trains to Deansgate and back, to protect the street crossings each journey, and assist as required"

Crook St. Dep.	06.15	07.00	07.45	13.00	14.00 SX	17.30 SX
Deansgate Arr.	06.30	07.15	08.00	13.10	14.10 SX	17.45 SX

Deansgate Dep.	06.45	07.30	08.15	13.30	14.30 SX	18.00 SX
Crook St. Arr.	07.00	07.45	08.30	13.45	14.45 SX	18.15 SX

The timings of these trains varied little over the years, the above times still being in place in 1922. In 1920 it was decreed that only two 'competent men' would normally be required to accompany the train, but that four should be used during the hours of darkness and during foggy weather and falling snow. The load limit on the branch was set at 16 wagons per trip for all trains except the 08.15 and 13.30 from Deansgate, for which the limit was raised to 25.

Information on early shunting and trip workings is scarce, but fortunately, a copy of the shunting and trip working diagram book for October 1920 has survived, and the details are reproduced below

Details of Shunting and Trip Workings, London and North Western Railway

Lancashire Area

October 1920 until further notice

<u>Bolton District Shunting Engines, Bolton Goods Yard and Sidings</u>

<u>No. 65</u>	Special Tank Shunting Engine
	6.00am to 1.00pm daily
	Also works trips as required, Crook St. Yard - Deansgate
<u>No. 66</u>	Special Tank Shunting Engine
	1.00pm - 2.00am SX
	11.30am - 4.00pm SO
	Also works trips as required, Crook St. Yard - Deansgate
<u>No. 67</u>	Special Tank Shunting Engine
	2.00am - 9.15am MX
	Shunts in Bolton Yard until 7.00am. Works 7.00am trip, Bolton to Plodder Lane
<u>No. 68</u>	Special Tank Shunting Engine
	7.00am - 7.30pm daily
	To shunt Lever St. sidings and work 8.15am trip Bolton to Lever St. Sidings.
	Works trips between Hulton Sidings, Plodder Lane, Crook St. and Deansgate as required.
<u>No. 69</u>	4-Cylinder Compound Engine
	(Atherton Banking and Shunting Engine)
	5.30am Monday to 6.00am Sunday
	Shunts Goods Yard and Up and Down Sidings and assists trains up and down Chequerbent Bank. Shunts as required Chequerbent Goods Yard.
<u>No. 70</u>	Spare

Bolton District Trip Engines

No. 71   Coal Tender Engine
               5.30am to 11.45am MO
               3.50am to 10.30am MX

	MO		MX	
	Arr	Dep	Arr	Dep
Plodder Lane Loco shed	-	5.30 Lt. eng	-	3.50 Light engine
Bolton	5.35	5.40	3.55	4.00 Light engine
Rumworth & Daubhill	5.45	7.10	4.10	6.20
Hulton Sidings	7.15	7.20	6.25	6.45
Chequerbent	7.25	7.30	6.50	7.00
Hulton Sidings	7.35	7.40	7.05	7.40
Rumworth & Daubhill	7.50	8.35	7.50	8.35
Hulton Sidings	8.40	9.15	8.40	9.15
Rumworth & Daubhill	9.20	9.45	9.20	9.45 Light engine
Bolton	9.55	10.10		
Hulton Sidings	10.20	11.10		
Bolton	11.30	11.35 Lt. eng		
Plodder Lane Loco Shed	11.45		10.30	

Shunts Goods Yard and Hulton Colliery Sdgs. at Rumworth and Daubhill

Plate 49. A L&NWR 0-8-0, probably on trip duties from Patricroft, is working 'engine plus van' at Hulton Sidings signalbox in August 1955. The site of the Hulton brick works, once served by a siding connection to the up line, is identified by the chimney in the background. The engine is not on the running lines, but is on the easternmost track that was the original formation of the Bolton and Leigh Railway.

                                                             Photo, G.J.Hardy.

No. 72   Coal Tender Engine
                6.00am to 7.20pm

	Arr	Dep
Plodder Lane Loco Shed	-	6.00 Light Engine
Atherton	6.20	7.00
*Chequerbent Bank	7.10	7.30
Atherton	7.40	8.15
Kenyon	8.40	9.30
Atherton	10.00	10.50
Chequerbent Bank	11.00	11.15
Hulton Sidings	11.30	12.45pm
Bolton Yard	1.00	1.30 Engine & Van
Atherton	1.45**	7.00 Light Engine
Plodder lane Loco Shed	7.20	

(re-manned at 1.00pm)
** To shunt and work trips between Atherton and Chequerbent Bank, also to shunt Atherton Goods yard 5pm to 7pm
(* Originally the printed instructions were to work 6am to 7.10am as above, and then 'work as required on the Bolton Branch to order of Control'. Due back at Plodder Lane at 1.00pm. The rest of the diagram was added in handwriting)

Plate 50. Class 5 4-6-0 No.45259, with a train of coal wagons has left Crook St., and is heading for Daubhill on the 1885 deviation route. The photograph was taken from Higher Swan Lane bridge looking towards Bolton on 15th. May 1953.

Photo, C.B.Golding.

No. 73   Coal Tender Engine
                7.10am to 2.10pm

	Arr	Dep
Plodder Lane Loco Shed	-	7.10 Light Engine
Kenyon	7.30am	

Works trips Kenyon to Hulton Sidings, Scowcroft's Sidings, Tyldesley and Astley Green as ordered by Control Office

Plate 51. On an occasion when Bolton Wanderers were playing an away game, (extra coaches were used on days of home games) Class 4 2-6-0 No.43029, leaves Daubhill for Bolton on 9th. May 1953. The station at Rumworth & Daubhill, closed by the time of this photograph, was located on the right hand curve just visible underneath the overbridge.

        Photo, C.B.Golding.

Plate 52. In earlier years passenger trains from Bolton would have shut off steam at this point for the stop at Rumworth & Daubhill, but LM&SR 2-6-2T No.41214 was able to keep the regulator open on the 1 in 60 climb as the station had closed the previous year. 41214 was working a two-coach motor train from Bolton Gt. Moor St. to Kenyon Jn. on 9th May 1953, and is seen here about 200 yards east of the former Rumworth & Daubhill station.

        Photo, C.B.Golding.

No. 74   Coal Tender Engine
              2.20pm to 9.20pm SX
              12.00 noon to 7.30pm SO

| | | SX |
	Arr	Dep
Plodder Lane Loco Shed	-	2.20
Chequerbent Bank	2.45	3.25
Atherton	3.30	3.45
Fletcher's Siding	3.55	4.10
West Leigh	4.20	4.40
Kenyon	5.00	5.30
West Leigh	5.40	5.50
Atherton	6.00	6.10
Chequerbent Bank	6.20	6.45
Atherton	6.55	7.45
Hulton Sidings	7.55	8.25
Bolton	8.45	9.05 Light Engine
Plodder Lane Loco Shed	9.20	

Plate 53. On 7th. July 1956, Class 5 4-6-0 No.44827 heads an excursion train to North Wales out of Bolton Gt. Moor St. station. The engine is on the crossover at the top of the ramp to the station; visible on the right are the hydraulic accumulator tower for the Crook St. warehouse, and behind it, the water tank at Gt. Moor St. station. To the left of the engine is the top floor of the three-story Crook St. goods warehouse.

Photo, C.B.Golding.

	SO	
	Arr	Dep
Plodder lane Loco Shed	-	12.00
Chequerbent Bank	12.20	1.20
Atherton	1.30	2.00
Chequerbent Bank	2.10	2.40
Atherton	2.50	3.20 Engine & Van
Chanter's Sidings	3.30	4.10
Atherton	4.25	5.00 Engine & Van
Fletcher's Sidings	5.10	5.20
Atherton	5.30	6.00
Chequerbent Bank	6.10	6.20
Hulton Sidings	6.30	6.40
Bolton	7.00	7.10 Light Engine
Plodder Lane Loco Shed	7.25	

45290? 45294 ? loc PATICROFT. LOCO FROM 1955

Plate 54, An unidentified Class 5 4-6-0, reporting No.W596, having passed Swan Lane Mill, makes its way toward Daubhill with a nine coach excursion to North Wales from Bolton Gt Moor St. on 29th June 1957. A train of this length would tax the facilities at Bolton. With a locomotive at the station end of the train, even in the longest platforms (2 or 3) the last coach would be off the end of the platform ramp.

only 2. Black 5's allocated to Paticroft. at this time the other one 45290. the last number is not a "O"

Photo, C.B.Golding.

<u>No. 75</u>   4-Cylinder Compound Engine
                 2.30pm to 9.10pm SX

	SX	
	<u>Arr</u>	<u>Dep</u>
Plodder Lane Loco Shed		2.30
Plodder Lane Yard	2.35	2.45
Lever St.	2.50	3.10
Bolton	3.15	3.25
Hulton Sidings	3.35	4.05
Fletcher's Sidings	4.20	5.00
Atherton	5.10	5.20
Chanter's Sidings	5.30	6.10
Atherton	6.20	7.40
Hulton Sidings	8.00	8.30
Bolton	8.50	9.05 Light Engine
Plodder Lane Loco Shed	9.10	

Conveys coal for Fletcher Burrows and Co.'s Depot and Hulton's Collieries Depot, High Level, Bolton

<u>No. 76</u>   Coal Tender Engine
                 6.20pm to 12.50am SX

	SX	
	<u>Arr</u>	<u>Dep</u>
Plodder Lane Loco Shed	-	6.20
Little Hulton	6.25	7.20
Bolton	7.55	8.10
Hulton Sidings	8.30	8.50
Chequerbent	8.55	9.10
Atherton	9.20	11.30
(shunts as required at Atherton)		
Hulton Sidings	11.50	12.15am
Bolton	12.30	12.45 Light Engine
Plodder Lane Loco Shed	12.50	

No. 77   Coal Tender Engine
                6.45pm to 1.50am SX
                6.55pm to 2.00am SO

	SX		SO	
	Arr	Dep	Arr	Dep
Plodder Lane Loco Shed	-	6.45	-	6.55
Bolton	7.00	7.10	7.00	8.00
Hulton Sidings	7.20	7.40		
Chequerbent Bank	7.45	8.00		
Hulton Sidings	8.15	10.50		
Bolton	11.05	12.15		
Little Hulton Jn.	12.25	12.45	8.15	8.30
Plodder Lane	12.50*	1.00	8.35	9.00
Bolton	1.10	1.40 LE	9.15	10.15
Hulton Sidings			10.30	10.50
Bolton			11.05	11.35
Hulton Sidings			11.45	12.25am
Bolton			12.45	1.30
Plodder Lane			1.40	1.55 Light Engine
Plodder Lane Loco Shed	1.50		2.00	

* To be re-manned at Plodder Lane at 12.55am

Plate 55. On 15th. March 1958, L&NWR 0-8-0 No.48926 has just collected some loaded coal wagons from the exchange sidings at Walkden, and reversed them onto its train, which was standing on the down line. The locomotive is blowing off steam in readiness for its attack on the 1 in 60 gradient ahead. The first move was to draw the train clear of the crossover so that the banking engine, just arrived from Plodder Lane on the up line, could move onto to rear.   Photo, G.Hayes.

Plate 56. At the rear of the train in the previous photograph, another L&NWR 0-8-0, No.49398, also with a full head of steam, has just buffered up to the guard's van. Walkden Sidings signalbox is seen in the background alongside the up (Manchester) line.

Photo, G.Hayes.

No. 78   Coal Tender Engine
             2.00pm to 9.00pm SO

	SO	
	Arr	Dep
Plodder Lane Loco Shed	-	2.00
Plodder Lane Yard	2.05	2.30
Bolton	2.40	3.10
Hulton Sidings	3.20	4.05
Atherton	4.20	5.00
Fletcherís Sidings	5.05	5.10
West Leigh Branch	5.20	5.35
Kenyon	5.45	then work to Control orders

No. 79   Coal Tender Engine
             7.00pm to 1.15am SO

	SO	
	Arr	Dep
Plodder Lane Loco Shed	-	7.00
Hulton Sidings	7.15	7.30
Chequerbent	7.35	7.45
Atherton	8.00	8.20
Kenyon	8.43	11.40 shunts as required
Atherton	11.50	12.05am
Hulton Sidings	12.20	12.35
Bolton	12.55	1.05 Light Engine
Plodder Lane Loco Shed	1.15	

Plate 57. At Little Hulton Jn. on 21st. September 1963, Class 3F 0-6-0T No.47378 runs around the stock of the LCGB 'South Lancashire Ltd.' Railtour. The coaches are on the Little Hulton Mineral Branch, and the tracks on the left, which once led to Little Hulton and Manchester, have been out of use since 1960. The signal box was retained as a ground frame until June 1966, but was already devoid of window glass at the time of this photograph. The up line to Manchester has been disconnected, but the down line is still intact at this point.

Photo, J. Marshall.

Plate 58. On 21St. September 1963, the LCGB's 'South Lancashire Ltd.' Railtour had reached Bolton from Manchester, Liverpool Rd. via Atherton. The six-coach train, headed by Class 8F 2-8-0 No.48178, was not able to use Gt. Moor St. station but stopped on the ramp from Fletcher St. The apparent gradient of the ramp is deceptive. It was indeed uphill, but only at 1 in 200. It appears much steeper as Crook St. yard falls away from Fletcher St. bridge, seen at the end of the train, on a downgrade of 1 in 154. Visible behind the train is the bulk of the Bridgeman St. goods warehouse.   Photo, Author.

No. 80   5ft. 6in. Passenger Engine
              7.55am to 10.15am MX

	MX	
	Arr	Dep
Kenyon (off 7.30am passenger		
from Bolton to Kenyon)	7.55	8.40
Bickershaw	8.55	9.10
Abram	9.15	9.30
Scowcroft's	9.40	10.00 Light Engine
Springs Branch Loco Shed	10.15	

Plate 59. Class 8F 2-8-0 No.48178 recouples to the stock of the LCGB 'South Lancashire Ltd.' Railtour at Fletcher St., Bolton, on 21st. September 1963, after the train had been taken to Little Hulton Jn. and back hauled by 3F 0-6-0T No.47378. It was a damp and murky day, typical of the area, and steam lingers from the train engine and from another 8F 2-8-0 in the sidings of Crook St. yard. Photo, Author.

Plate 60. Bolton Gt. Moor St. station, viewed from the end-loading dock, on the last day of passenger services, 27th. March 1954. The 2-6-2 Tank locomotive is standing just off the end of platform 1.

Photo, Author's collection.

Classification of Sidings

Scowcroft's	7 sidings. Total capacity 200 wagons (see note)
Bolton	16 sidings including through road to Deansgate and a cattle dock. Total capacity 357 wagons
Hulton Sidings	4 sidings. Total capacity 126 wagons
Lever St.	4 sidings. Total capacity 112 wagons
Kenyon	11 sidings. 1 siding used for stabling passenger stock Total capacity 432 wagons
Atherton	4 sidings plus a loop (up side). Total capacity 180 wagons 4 sidings down side. Total capacity 93 wagons
West Leigh	2 sidings. Total capacity 80 wagons

Note: The Scowcroft's siding referred to in this document was located between Hindley and Pennington.

Plate 61. The last passenger train on the L&NWR lines in the Bolton area was this two-brakevan special, organised by the LCGB on 9th. May 1964. The train is seen here in the yard at Crook St. on its way to the Magee, Marshall's Siding on the High St. branch, propelled by Class. 3F 0-6-0T No.47378.

Photo, Dr.J.G.Blears.

This remarkable document provides invaluable detail, not only of the shunting and trip workings from Plodder Lane shed, but also of the engines used for them. Although it comes from a relatively late date (1920) it is surely representative of similar duties from earlier times: indeed, given that static nature of the locomotive allocation at Plodder Lane for many years prior to 1920, the details of the locomotives would not be inappropriate for the nineteenth century. Particularly notable is trip working no. 69, as it provides details of the banking engine stationed at Atherton. This was undoubtedly a well established working by this time, and was to remain a feature until the end of steam operation on that section, although the locomotive concerned was provided by Patricroft sheds in later years. Also notable is the fact that almost all the trip workings took place around the Bolton - Kenyon area, with only the occasional trip to Little Hulton Jn and no analogous workings to Walkden, for example.

There were some adjustments to the trip workings over the years as traffic flows changed, but trips from Plodder Lane continued to follow a similar pattern until the 1940's. The trip 'targets', rectangular pieces of metal with the trip number painted on the front and a loop on the rear for placing over a lamp bracket on the engine, were held in a rack at the shed, although they were not used in the later years.

Trip workings were not shown in the regular working timetables of the period, nor was another operation that visited Plodder Lane on a regular basis, the stores train from St. Helens Jn. that carried station supplies (oil, stores, etc.), wagon sheets and tarpaulins. St. Helens Jn. served the entire L&NWR system in a series of monthly trains one of which (in 1921) was a two-day operation to supply stations along the following route: day one (06.23 to 19.19), St. Helens - Liverpool Lime St. - Stockport - Diggle - Huddersfield - Copley Hill - Morley (Leeds); day two Morley - Huddersfield - Oldham - Plodder Lane - Bolton - Kenyon (also unloading supplies for Tyldesley and Leigh) - St. Helens. The train was scheduled to call at Plodder Lane between 12.28 and 12.50, during which 'time allowed for engine to turn. Train to shunt for 12.05 Manchester to Bolton', and at Bolton from 12.56 to 13.55. This would involve tender-first working from Plodder Lane to Bolton, and smokebox-first working down the Chequerbent incline, the latter needing careful work to maintain the water level in the firebox.

Plate 62. A Patricroft shed (10C) locomotive, LM&SR 2-6-2T No.207, takes the Bolton road at Roe Green Jn. with an evening Manchester to Bolton local passenger train in August 1946. The train is composed of the 3-coach set which was standard for this service.
Photo, J.H.Tonge

LOCAL PASSENGER WORKINGS, 1874-1922 .

The initial passenger services between Bolton Great Moor Street and Manchester were worked by Patricroft engines, as the new facilities at Plodder Lane were not ready in time for the opening of the line to passengers, and Patricroft engines continued to work a substantial proportion of these services until their cessation in 1954. From the start of its life, however, Plodder Lane shed took over responsibility for the bulk of the Bolton - Tyldesley - Leigh - Warrington - St. Helens services, an area in which it continued to operate until closure. The passenger timetables for April 1875, the first month in which services on the direct Bolton - Manchester route were provided, show ten weekday trains from Bolton to Kenyon, with eleven in the opposite direction, and a Sunday service of four trains each way. The Manchester line had no Sunday service,

but 10 trains each way on weekdays and Saturdays, two of which ran to and from London Road station in Manchester, the remainder using Victoria station. The first departure from Bolton, the 'government' train at 07.00, arrived in Victoria at 07.40 while the last train of the day, the 21.30 from Bolton, reached the same destination at 22.10. Trains to Bolton ran to similar times, the first down train (again a 'government' train) leaving Victoria at 06.50 to arrive in Bolton at 07.30. Every down train stopped at all the stations on the Little Hulton Branch, but interestingly three of the up trains missed out the Plodder Lane stop, running non-stop from Bolton to Little Hulton before proceeding on to Manchester. The following fares from Manchester Victoria were quoted in the May 1875 issue of Bradshaw's Railway Guide:

	Single				Return		
To	1st.	2nd.	3rd.	Gov.	1st.	2nd.	3rd.
Worsley	0/9	0/7	0/5½	0/5	1/3	1/0	0/11
Walkden	1/1	0/10	0/7½	0/7	1/10	1/5	1/0
Little Hulton	1/3	0/11	0/8½	0/8	2/1	1/7	1/2
Plodder Lane	1/6	1/1	0/10	0/9½	2/6	1/10	1/5
Bolton	2/0	1/6	0/11½	0/10½	3/0	2/0	1/6

To put these rates into context, cotton spinners working in Bolton in 1875, a period of economic stability and vigorous trade, would have earned around £3/10/0 weekly, bringing the occasional trip to Manchester, at least by 3rd. class travel, well within their means.

The pattern of train services on the Little Hulton line rapidly took on the shape it was to assume for the next 40 years until the cutbacks of the 1940's began. In 1890, 15 years after opening, the passenger service was little changed from that of 1875; a daily London train had been added, the new Exchange station was now the favoured destination in Manchester, Plodder Lane carried a timetable footnote reading 'station for Farnworth', and another innovation was a single early morning short trip from Bolton to Little Hulton, returning from

Walkden at midday, but otherwise the service of eleven up and twelve down trains was remarkably similar to that of the opening day. By 1900, the description "Plodder Lane for Farnworth" appeared in full in both public and working timetables.

On the Kenyon line a pattern of service also began to emerge that would also continue essentially unchanged until the second world war, consisting of a series of Bolton-Atherton-Tyldesley-Leigh-Kenyon Jn. trains (and their counterparts in the reverse direction) superimposed on a series of direct Bolton-Kenyon Jn. trains, some of which would continue to Warrington or St. Helens. In 1890, for example, there were seven trains daily each way between Bolton and Kenyon Junction via Tyldesley, and three additional trains from Bolton to Tyldesley that continued on to Manchester Exchange, and eight trains running daily directly from Bolton to Kenyon Jn., with a reduced service on Sundays. The Bolton to Manchester via Tyldesley trains, relics of the days before the Little Hulton Extension Railway was completed, and the through trains from Bolton to Warrington and St. Helens, were still running in January 1900 but all had disappeared from the timetables by the summer of 1904, by which time the Bolton to St. Helens and Warrington trains had been cut back to terminate at Earlestown. Several of the through Warrington trains re-appeared in the timetables by 1910, but the direct service to St. Helens was not revived until 1935.

In December 1922, on the eve of the grouping that saw the lines in question become part of the London, Midland & Scottish Railway, the local passenger services had changed little from those of earlier years. Twelve trains ran daily each way on the Bolton Gt. Moor St. to Manchester Line, an 06.30 departure in each direction starting the day which finished with the 21.45 SO departure from Bolton to Manchester and the 22.10 in the return direction. In addition, five trains now ran each way only between Bolton and Monton Green, but this line still saw no services on Sundays. The Atherton route was used by a total of 17 daily passenger trains, from the 05.50 Bolton to Kenyon Jn. via Tyldesley to the 22.58 arrival at Bolton directly from Kenyon Jn. via West Leigh, and still had a minimal service on Sundays.

Plate 63. One of the long-lived Webb designed, ex L&NW 'Coal Tanks' is seen in the vicinity of Eccles c1946, working a Manchester Exchange- Bolton Great Moor St. local service.

Photo, D.Evans.

THROUGH TRAINS TO LONDON

At the time of opening of the Little Hulton branch there was no through service from Bolton to London, but the L&NWR were not long in taking advantage of their new route from Bolton to offer through trains to the capital. The date on which they commenced is not clear, but by the summer of 1880 two daily through services were in place, shown in the timetable as operating via Manchester London Road as follows (Sundays excepted):

Up Trains					Down Trains				
Bolton Gt. Moor St.	Dep.	08.25	15.00		London Euston	Dep.	10.00	14.45
Manchester L.R.	Arr.	09.10	15.52		Manchester L.R.	Arr.	14.40	19.30
	Dep.	09.30	16.00			Dep.	15.05	19.45
London Euston	Arr.	14.15	21.00		Bolton Gt. Moor St.	Arr.	15.59	20.53

A note in the summer 1880 public timetable reads 'Bolton and London tickets are available via Manchester or Warrington, but if used via Manchester the passengers will cross from one station to the other at their own expense unless they travel by the through trains between Bolton and London Road.' As most Bolton trains were using Victoria station in Manchester at this time, this would have involved considerable inconvenience, a situation familiar to travellers between Bolton and London well into the modern era, until the opening of the Salford link gave direct access from Bolton Trinity St. to Manchester Piccadilly. The note and times suggest that through carriages to and from Bolton, at least for the morning trains, may have been shunted to and from London trains at Manchester London Road station. This would clearly have involved some inconvenient movements from the through platforms on the Oxford Road line to the terminal roads at London Road. There is no indication at any time that the Bolton to London through trains were anything more than through carriages, added to London-bound trains at an appropriate intermediate station. The restriction of 13 vehicles into and out of Bolton Gt. Moor St. station that appeared in the appendices to the working timetables throughout the period of the through London trains was undoubtedly referring to movement of local stock.

By 1890 the through service to London via Manchester had been reduced to one daily train in each direction, Sundays excepted, running to the following times:

Up Trains			Down Trains	
Bolton Gt. Moor St.	Dep.	10.30	London Euston	Dep.	12.00
Worsley		10.42	Manchester London Rd.		16.30
Eccles		10.46	Manchester Oxford Rd.		16.32
Ordsall Lane		10.52	Ordsall Lane		16.37
Manchester Oxford Rd.		10.57	Eccles		16.43
Manchester London Rd.		11.00	Worsley		16.48
London Euston	Arr.	15.30	Walkden		16.52
			Little Hulton		16.56
			Plodder Lane*		16.50
			Bolton Gt. Moor St.	Arr.	16.56

* Station for Farnworth

89

It is noteworthy that, while the down train stopped at all stations along the Little Hulton line to set down passengers from south of Macclesfield on notice being given to the guard, no official provision was originally made for passengers to join the up train from these stations. In the early years of the service passengers to London from these stations made use of an unofficial arrangement whereby, provided they arrived at their local station before the train left Bolton, they could notify the station staff of their intention to travel to London and a call to Bolton would ensure that the engine crew would stop the train to pick them up. By 1910, however, this arrangement was officially sanctioned and a note in the passenger timetables advised intending passengers of the procedure. In addition to the through carriages to London via Manchester, passengers in 1890 also had the option of travelling directly from Bolton Gt. Moor St. to London via Kenyon Junction and Warrington, by choosing the following trains:

Up Train			Down Trains		
Bolton Gt. Moor St. Dep.	13.25		London Euston Dep.	13.15	14.00
Rumworth & Daubhill	13.29		Kenyon Jn.	18.11	18.42
Chequerbent	13.33		West Leigh	18.16	18.47
Atherton	13.38		Atherton	18.22	18.53
West Leigh	13.43		Chequerbent	-	-
Kenyon Jn.	13.47		Rumworth & Daubhill	-	-
London Euston Arr.	18.25		Bolton Gt. Moor St. Arr.	18.30	19.00

Although the through service to London via Manchester had been reduced by this time, good connections to London from Bolton and the intermediate stations to Manchester were still available by using the trains that ran directly from Gt. Moor St. station to Manchester London Road.

By 1900 however, the through trains via Warrington had been discontinued, but in addition to the through train each way via Manchester, connections were advertised by changing at London Road as shown below:

Up Trains		#	*	Down Trains		*	#
Bolton Gt. Moor St.	Dep.	09.05	11.10	London Euston	Dep.	12.00	17.30
Manchester London Rd. Arr.		09.50		Manchester London Rd. Arr.			21.45
	Dep.	10.00			Dep.		22.00
London Euston	Arr.	14.20	16.15	Bolton Gt. Moor St.	Arr.	16.57	22.45

* Through carriages
# Stopping train to Manchester London Road

In 1900, connections were also advertised between Bolton and London Euston and Bolton and Birmingham New St. by changing at Stockport, and travelling via Droylsden and Manchester Exchange, but journeys by the latter route took longer than by the direct cross-Manchester trains. By the turn of the century the through carriages from Bolton to London were being worked to Stockport and attached to a Manchester - London express there.

By 1910 through L&NWR services between Bolton and London had been increased, but only one up train used Gt. Moor St. station, most trains operating from Bolton L&YR (Trinity St.) station according to the following timetable: (page 91)

Up Trains				
Bolton Gt. Moor St.	Dep.	-	11.26	-
Bolton Trinity St.	Dep.	09.32	-	13.30
London Euston	Arr.	14.10	16.00	18.10

Down Trains				
London Euston	Dep.	10.30	16.05	18.05
Bolton Trinity St.	Arr.	14.47	20.53	22.14
Bolton Gt. Moor St.	Arr.	-		

The trains to and from Trinity St. station also provided a service for East Lancashire, and ran via Manchester Victoria. The L&NWR Marshalling Circular for October 1913 records that a single 57ft brake composite from Bolton Gt. Moor St. was attached to the 12.10pm corridor train, Manchester - London via Colwich at Stockport. The coach returned the next day on the 5.00am service to Manchester, then was worked locally to Stockport and back before proceeding to Bolton at 3.45pm for the next days service to London. It is not surprising that the coach was not returned to Bolton directly on a corresponding down through working from Euston as all such trains used the L&YR route to Trinity St. station by this time. The through carriages between Bolton Great Moor St. and London ceased to operate during the first World War, never to be reinstated, and the local train service from Bolton was concentrated on Manchester Exchange. As late as the British Railways era in 1948, however, the ABC Railway Guide's listing for Bolton included, in addition to trains from Trinity St. station, details of connection from Gt. Moor St. station to London, but by this late date only via Kenyon Jn. and Warrington.

Plate 64. Little remains of Kenyon Junction station in this late 1960's view in the 'Up' direction, the days of connections from Bolton Great Moor St. to Euston but a memory. The once busy yard at Kenyon had seen its last freight, only the occasional sludge train using the rusting metals.   Photo, P.Hampson.

Plate 65. Class 5 4-6-0 No.45026 with a returning eight-coach excursion form North Wales, climbing Chequerbent bank with rear-end assistance on 7th July 1956. The banking engine has just cleared the steepest part of the incline, but the train engine is still working hard and blowing off excess steam. Photo, C.B.Golding.

Plate 66. A view of shunting in operation at Bolton Gt. Moor St., in charge of an unidentified L&NWR 2-4-2T. Although the photograph is undated, it was taken prior to the shortening of the overall roof in 1930/31. Movements from the station are controlled by two L&NWR bracket signals, which indicate that a train is due to depart from platform 3. These signals were replaced by starter signals on individual posts during the 1940's. The constriction by Crook St. bridge of the access to the station is apparent in this view, taken from the approach ramp just south of Bolton No.1 signal box, the west wall of the bridge being visible on the left.

Photo, J.Marshall.

TRAINS AT PLODDER LANE, NOVEMBER 1918.

A compilation from the working timetables, Table 5, shows the extent of the traffic at Plodder Lane in November, 1918. This was truly a 24 hour operation; it should be recalled that the following list does not include light engine movements from the shed to and from Bolton or the Little Hulton Jn. direction.

Table 5 Traffic at Plodder Lane November 1918					
Train	From	Plodder Lane Arr.	Dep	To	Notes
Goods	Bolton	Pass	00.20	Little Hulton Jn.	SMX
Goods	Little Hulton Jn.	00.50	01.00	Bolton	MX
XP Goods	Ordsall Lane	02.20	02.30	Bolton	MX
Goods	Ship Canal Branch	04.15	04.30	Bolton	MX
Goods	Patricroft	-	05.30	Bolton	MO
Passenger	Monton Green	-	05.43	Bolton	
XP Goods	Longsight	Pass	05.50	Bolton	MX
Goods	Bolton	05.50	06.15	Highfield Sidings	MX. Mineral beyond Plodder Lane
Passenger	Bolton	-	06.03	Monton Green	
Passenger	Bolton	-	06.41	Manchester Ex.	
Passenger	Manchester Ex.	-	07.09	Bolton	
Passenger	Manchester Ex.	-	08.11	Bolton	
Passenger	Bolton	-	08.16	Manchester Ex.	
Passenger	Bolton	-	08.41	Manchester Ex.	
Passenger	Bolton	-	09.26	Manchester Ex.	
Passenger	Monton Green	-	09.53	Bolton	
Mineral	-	-	11.40	Little Hulton Jn.	Shunts Highfield Sidings 11.43-12.25
Goods	Ordsdall Lane	11.40	11.50	Bolton	
Passenger	Bolton	-	12.21	Monton Green	
Empty Goods	-	-	12.30	Edge Hill	Via Bolton
Mineral	Little Hulton Jn.	12.35			
Passenger	Manchester Ex.	-	12.50	Bolton	SX
Mineral	Highfield Sidings	13.05			
Passenger	Manchester Ex.	-	13.11	Bolton	SO
Mineral	Highfield Sidings	13.20			
Special Goods	Ordsall Lane	pass	13.22	Bolton	Includes cattle
Passenger	Bolton	-	13.32	Manchester Ex.	SX
Passenger	Monton Green	-	13.38	Bolton	SX
Passenger	Bolton	-	13.46	Manchester Ex.	SO

Train	From	Plodder Lane Arr.	Dep	To	Notes
Mineral	-	-	13.50	Highfield Sidings	
Passenger	Monton Green	-	14.08	Bolton	SO
Empty Mineral	-	-	14.30	Kenyon Jn.	SO To Fletcher Burrows Chanters Colliery, Atherton, via Bolton
Empty Mineral	-	-	14.45	Kenyon Jn.	SX To Fletcher Burrows Chanters Colliery, Atherton, via Bolton.
Mineral	Patricroft	15.15	-	-	SO
Engine & Van	-	-	15.30	Sanderson's Sidings	SO To work as below, arriving Plodder Lane 17.00
Mineral	Patricroft	15.40	-	-	SX
Mineral	Bolton	Pass	16.00	Kenyon Jn. via Roe Green Jn.	Shunts Highfield as required.
Empty Goods	-	-	16.00	Edge Hill via Bolton	SX
Passenger	Bolton	-	16.21	Monton Green	SX
Goods	Bolton	Pass	16.35	Little Hulton Jn.	Calls at Highfield Sidings.
Passenger	Manchester Ex.	-	16.56	Bolton	
Mineral	Sanderson's Siding	17.00	-	-	SO
Mineral	Sanderson's Siding	17.30	-	-	SX
Engine & Van	-	-	17.45	Little Hulton Jn.	SO
Passenger	Bolton	-	17.56	Manchester Ex	
Passenger	Manchester Ex.	-	17.58	Bolton	
Passenger	Monton Green	-	18.51	Bolton	SX
Empty Mineral	Bolton	19.12	-	-	SX
Mineral	Little Hulton Jn.	19.25	19.45	Bolton	SX
Fast Goods	Bolton	Pass	19.35	Patricroft	
Passenger	Bolton	-	21.01	Manchester Ex.	
Fast Goods	Bolton	Pass	21.10	Patricroft	Extended to Cross Lane as required.
Passenger	Manchester Ex.	-	22.02	Bolton	
Mineral	Atherton via Bolton	22.15	-	-	
Goods	Ordsall Lane	Pass	22.30	Bolton	SO
Mineral	Bolton	Pass	23.05	Little Hulton Jn.	
Mineral	-	-	23.35	Bolton	SX

The intensity of operations from Bolton in both the Little Hulton and Atherton directions can also be judged from the opening times of the key signal boxes along the lines. In 1904, for example, Bolton No. 2 (Fletcher St. Junction) box was open on a 24 hour day, 7 day week basis, while the closing times for other key boxes were: Plodder Lane No. 2, from 04.00 Sundays to 05.00 Mondays; Little Hulton Jn. from 02.00 Sundays to 06.00 Mondays; and Hulton Sidings from 04.00 on Sundays to 05.30 on Mondays. In the same period, other boxes along both lines that handled only through train movements, such as Plodder Lane No. 1, and those such as Rumworth & Daubhill and Bolton No. 1 that controlled only passenger or local freight trips, were also closed overnight, in the case of the latter box for example from 00.00 to 04.00. At times when all the intermediate boxes were closed, the routes from Fletcher St. Jn. to Howe Bridge East Jn., and from Fletcher St. Jn. to Roe Green Jn., were designated as single block sections.

Plate 67. One of the celebrated L&NW 'Coal Tanks' No.7789 is seen passing Sanderson's Sidings signal box with the auto set working a Manchester Exchange-Bolton Great Moor St. service in the spring of 1947.

Photo, W.D.Cooper.

FREIGHT WORKINGS DURING LM&SR DAYS, 1923-1947

The pattern of freight workings established by the L&NWR continued unchanged for some time after the formation of the LM&SR in 1923, but by the end of the period under review the number of trains had been reduced. The Little Hulton line, for example, showed the following pattern of trains, including some light engine movements, in the summer of 1939 (Tables 6 and 7). Light engine movements in connection with passenger services at this time will be dealt with later.

Table 6. Extract from LM&SR working timetables May 1st. to September 24th. 1939, Freight trains, Up Line

		MO		SX		SO	SX			SO	SX	SX	SO
Bolton	Dep.		06.35		10.26				14.55				21.40	21.40
Fletcher St. Jn			*06.37*		*10.29*				*14.58*			*21.43*	
Lever St.	Arr.				10.36				15.01				
	Dep.								15.11				
Plodder Lane	Arr.		06.45									21.53	21.50
	Dep.	03.30	07.45	09.25		11.00	12.25	13.57		16.45	18.50	22.07	
Highfield Sidings	Arr.		07.09			11.04	12.30	14.00					
	Dep.					11.40	13.20						
Little Hulton Jn.	Arr.					11.45	13.25		15.19	16.50	18.55	22.14	
	Dep.								15.28	17.15	19.33	22.32	
Walkden Sidings	Arr.								15.33				
	Dep.												
Roe Green Jn.				*09.46*							*17.27*	*19.46*	*22.44*	
Notes		A	B	C			B		D	E	F	G	H

Passing times shown in italics
A: LE to work 04.20 Ordsall Lane to Bolton
B: runs as required, Plodder Lane to Highfield Sidings
C: runs as required. To Patricroft arrive 09.54
D: stops at Plodder Lane for traffic purposes when required
E: to Stott Lane Sidings (Eccles)
F: engine and brake to Patricroft
G: through freight to Ordsall Lane
H: LE after working the 19.20 Kenyon to Bolton

Table 7. Extract from LM&SR working timetables May 1st. to September 24th. 1939, Freight trains, Down Line

		MX	MX	MX	MO		SO	SX	SX			SO
Roe Green Jn.		*04.08*	*04.24*	*04.59*	*05.02*				*12.53*			*15.04*
Walkden Sidings	Arr.								12.59			15.10
	Dep.								13.09			15.29
Little Hulton Jn.	Arr.								13.19			15.39
	Dep.						12.53	13.41	13.56			16.20
Highfield Sidings	Arr.											
	Dep.											
Plodder Lane	Arr.		04.24	04.37	05.09	05.19	12.28	13.46		14.30		16.25
	Dep.	03.40	04.33		05.37					14.32	15.00	
Lever St.	Arr.									14.37	15.05	
	Dep.					10.05				14.52	15.15	
Fletcher St. Jn.		*03.46*	*04.40*		*05.44*	*10.08*			*14.10*	*14.54*	*15.18*	
Bolton	Arr.	03.48	04.43		05.47	10.11			14.12	14.56	15.20	
		A	B	C	D	E	F	F	G	H	I	J

		SX	SO	SX	SX	SO
Roe Green Jn.					*16.48*	*16.48*
Walkden Sidings	Arr.				16.53	16.53
	Dep.	15.53	15.53		17.15	17.15
Little Hulton Jn.	Arr.	16.00			17.25	17.25
	Dep.		16.30		18.20	17.40
Highfield Sidings	Arr.					
	Dep.					
Plodder Lane	Arr.			16.35	18.25	17.45
	Dep.			17.15		
Lever St.	Arr.					
	Dep.					
Fletcher St. Jn.			*16.11*	*17.22*		
Bolton	Arr.			17.25		
		K	L		M	N

Passing times shown in italics

A: LE to Atherton

B: through freight from Ordsall Lane

C: runs as required. 04.10 LE from Tyldesley

D: 04.45 LE from Jackson's Siding

E: through freight from Ordsall Lane

F: empties

G: from Patricroft

H: mineral to Atherton. LE leaves shed at 14.28

I: mineral to Kenyon

J: mineral from Patricroft

K: mineral

L: engine and brake to Atherton

M: LE from Patricroft dep. 16.40 to Walkden, then mineral

N: 16.45 from Sanderson's Siding. Stops when required for traffic purposes at Roe Green Jn.

Comparison of the 1939 timetable for the Little Hulton line with those of earlier times shows how the through freight traffic has declined, leaving only one train to work five times a week from Bolton to Manchester (Ordsall Lane), with two working in the reverse direction, from Ordsall Lane and Patricroft. A number of trains connected the Manchester area with Plodder Lane, stopping to exchange traffic at Little Hulton Junction in both directions and Walkden in the down direction, but did not serve Bolton. However, Lever St. and Highfield Sidings were still well served by up trains, and the yard at Plodder Lane was well used, although not to capacity .

On the Atherton line the picture was similar, with local workings predominant, although a through Liverpool train continued to operate throughout the LM&SR period. In 1948 the locomotive for this train, usually an ex L&NWR 0-8-0 or LM&SR Class 4F 0-6-0, left Plodder Lane at 04.30 to work the 05.20MX Atherton to Edge Hill, arriving at 06.57, and returned with the 09.20 Edge Hill to Atherton. A daily departure for Wigan (Springs Branch) left Crook St. in the morning to run via Atherton, and Howe Bridge West Jn., but the return working ran via Golborne and Kenyon Jn.

Some additional details of freight train workings during this period on both the Little Hulton and Atherton lines have come to light in the sectional appendices to the LM&SR working timetables, and in that company's booklet 'Loading of Passenger and Freight Trains, Western Division', dated Oct. 1st. 1945. In all the categories listed in the latter document, the load restrictions between Atherton and Chequerbent were the most severe for any section of line. The loading of freight and mineral trains was expressed in a complex manner: rather than being specified in tons, loads were calculated in terms of wagon equivalents according to a formula based on the type of wagon involved. For example, 3½ wagons of goods or 5 empty wagons were considered equivalent to 2 mineral wagons, the standard unit of a 'mineral wagon' being defined as a loaded 13-ton wagon. Each wagon type or load was allotted an equivalent number of mineral wagons for the purposes of load calculation. For example a loaded 20-ton tank wagon was considered as being equivalent to 2 mineral wagons; an empty 50-ton Warflat or Warwell wagon was equivalent to 2 mineral wagons; a loaded sludge tender counted as 3 mineral wagons, while a large engine (not in steam) plus tender was specified for load purposes as 6 mineral wagons. Using this system, the loadings for express and through freight trains were specified as summarised in Table 8:

Plate 68. One of the Ivatt Class 2-6-2T's, No.41287, is seen at Pennington South Jn. working the 7.10pm (SX) Kenyon Jn.-Tyldesley local on 20th May 1958. After the demise of Plodder Lane shed, many of the local services were worked by Patricroft (26F) engines, 41287 being a regular performer.

Photo, Peter Johnson.

Table 8. Maximum loadings of Freight Trains, in wagons of goods+

Between	Type of Train	Up Trains							Down Trains						
		Class of Engine							Class of Engine						
		2	3	4	5	6	7	8	2	3	4	5	6	7	8
Kenyon and Bolton *	Express Freight	10	12	14	15	17	18	20	37	45	54	59	65	72	79
Kenyon and Bolton*	Through Freight	10	12	14	15	17	18	20	37	45	54	59	65	72	79
Bolton and Roe Green Jn.	Express Freight	31	37	45	50	54	60	66	20	24	30	32	36	40	44
Bolton and Roe Green Jn.	Through Freight	37	45	54	60	65	71	78	25	30	36	40	44	48	53

+ When traffic of the weight of mineral is conveyed by these trains, two such wagons must be reckoned as $3\frac{1}{2}$ wagons of goods.

* Maximum loads down Chequerbent bank were specified as:

For 1 engine and 1 goods guard - equal to 13 wagons of mineral

For 1 engine and 1 goods guard assisted by traffic shunter - equal to 22 wagons of mineral

For 2 engines and 1 goods guard assisted by traffic shunter - equal to 31 wagons of mineral

Plate 69. Daubhill Coal Yard in the 1950's with the Ex- Bolton & Leigh line on the extreme left. The crossing on St. Helens Road is visible and in the background is Sunnyside Mill's tower.

Photo, J.Jones.

The 'traffic shunter' referred to on page 99 was still described in the contemporary Appendix to the Working Timetable as a 'bank rider', the relevant section specifying that 'no train of over 13 loaded mineral wagons must travel down the incline from Chequerbent station to Atherton unless accompanied by a bank rider.'

The maximum allowable loading for mineral trains was specified more closely by section, resulting in a more flexible working arrangement (Table 9).

Table 9. Maximum Loadings of Mineral Trains, in mineral wagons

Between	Up Trains							Down Trains						
	Class of Engine							Class of Engine						
	2	3	4	5	6	7	8	2	3	4	5	6	7	8
Atherton and Hulton Sidings *	7	8	10	11	12	14	15	36	43	52	57	63	69	76
Hulton Sidings and Rumworth & Daubhill	23	27	33	36	40	44	48	22	26	31	34	38	41	45
Rumworth & Daubhill and Bolton	20	24	29	32	36	39	43	22	26	31	34	38	41	45
Bolton and Plodder Lane	22	26	31	34	38	41	45	26	32	38	42	46	51	56
Plodder Lane and Roe Green Jn.	26	32	38	42	46	51	56	16	19	22	25	27	30	33
Little Hulton Jn. and Little Hulton Colliery	22	26	31	34	38	41	45	22	26	31	34	38	41	45

* Banking only to be performed by class 6 or 7 engines: loads in the down direction subject to the maxima specified in Table 8

The description of the terminus of the Little Hulton branch as 'Little Hulton Colliery' used in Table 9 is reproduced from the LM&SR Loadings Booklet of 1945. In practice, no such establishment existed, and the Appendix to the Working Timetables contains the more accurate description of the limit of the branch as 'Roscoe's colliery'. The latter document, in addition to providing details for shunting procedures on the branch, instructs that, "when it is necessary for wagons to stand on the branch, care must be taken to leave the following occupation level crossings free:-
Hamnett's Crossing, 188 yards from Little Hulton Junction

Hodgkiss's Crossing, 524 yards do.
Kirkham's Crossing, 1,420 yards do.
Roscoe's Crossing, 1,610 yards do."

Banking of freight and mineral trains that exceeded the single engine load was also required between Roe Green Jn. and Plodder Lane but, unlike the Atherton to Chequerbent section, banking of passenger trains from Roe Green to Plodder Lane was not permitted. In the up direction, freight and mineral trains were to stop as necessary at the Little Hulton Jn. home signal to pin down brakes for the descent to Roe Green Jn.

PASSENGER WORKINGS DURING LM&SR DAYS, 1923-1947

Except for a reduction in numbers, the local passenger train service between Manchester and Bolton saw little change during this period. All Manchester trains now used Exchange station, and the short workings from Bolton to Monton Green continued to operate, usually as two-coach push-and-pull sets with the coal tank at the Manchester end. The off-peak through trains to Manchester had three-coach ordinary sets, increased to four coaches for the morning and evening trains. Engines could work either way round on the Manchester services, but only bunker first from Bolton to Kenyon to reduce the risk of exposing the firebox crown on Chequerbent incline. Plodder Lane was still a busy place, with passenger trains and associated light engine movements in July 1934 from 04.00 until after 23.00, as shown in Table 10.

Table 10. Passenger trains and associated light engine movements at Plodder Lane, July 1934

Train	From	Plodder Lane Arr	Plodder Lane Dep.	To	Notes
Light Engine			04.05	Leigh via Roe Green	SO To work 05.10 Leigh-Tyldesley.
Light Engine			04.55	Leigh via Roe Green	SX. To work 06.05 Leigh-Manchester Ex.
Light Engine			06.16	Tyldesley	
	Bolton		06.36	Manchester Ex.	
	Manchester Ex.		07.03	Bolton	
	Bolton		07.31	Manchester Ex.	
	Manchester Ex.		08.09	Bolton	
	Bolton		08.16	Manchester Ex.	
	Bolton		08.30	Manchester Ex.	
	Manchester Ex.		08.41	Bolton	
	Bolton		09.25	Manchester Ex.	
	Cross Lane		09.56	Bolton	
	Bolton		12.21	Monton Green	
	Monton Green		12.28	Bolton	SO (12.45SX.)
	Monton Green		12.58	Bolton	SO
	Bolton		13.31	Manchester Ex.	
	Monton Green		13.38	Bolton	SX
	Bolton		13.46	Manchester Ex.	SO
	Monton Green		14.08	Bolton	SO

Train	From	Plodder Lane Arr	Plodder Lane Dep.	To	Notes
	Bolton		14.26	Manchester Ex.	To Monton Green SO.
	Manchester Ex.		14.28	Bolton	SX
	Monton Green		14.37	Bolton	SO
	Bolton		15.33	Manchester Ex.	SO
	Bolton		15.38	Manchester Ex.	SX
	Manchester Ex.		15.55	Bolton	
	Bolton		16.21	Monton Green	SO
	Bolton		16.36	Manchester Ex.	SX
	Manchester Ex.		16.56	Bolton	
Light Engine	Tyldesley via Roe Green	17.00			
	Bolton		17.51	Manchester Ex.	
	Manchester Ex.		17.59	Bolton	
	Manchester Ex.		18.25	Bolton	SO
	Bolton		18.46	Manchester Ex.	
	Monton Green		18.49	Bolton	
Light Engine	Tyldesley via Roe Green	19.18			
	Manchester Ex.		19.44	Bolton	
Light Engine	Atherton	20.12			
	Bolton		20.26	Little Hulton	SO
Light Engine	Tyldesley	20.48			SO
	Walkden		21.00	Bolton	SO
	Bolton		21.01	Manchester Ex.	
	Bolton		21.19	Manchester Ex.	SO
	Manchester Ex.		21.27	Bolton	
	Bolton		22.06	Manchester Ex.	SO
	Bolton		22.21	Eccles	SX (see note opposite)
	Manchester Ex.		22.34	Bolton	
Light Engine	Tyldesley	23.00			
	Bolton		23.06	Manchester Ex.	
	Eccles		23.28	Bolton	SX (see note opposite)
	Manchester Ex.		23.41	Bolton	SO

Note: this train turns at Stott Lane Sidings, 1/2 mile beyond Eccles station, running ECS to and from Eccles.

One notable feature of this pattern of working was the continuation of the long-established SO service from Bolton to Little Hulton, which returned from Walkden, a consequence of the absence of a crossover at the former station requiring the use of Walkden Sidings for this purpose. The pattern of light engine working shown in Table 10 was repeated with minor variations in times and number of trips throughout the 1930's and early 1940's, with light engine movements to and from Tyldesley normally working via Roe Green, while those from Kenyon or Atherton worked via Bolton.

The light engine movements listed in Table 10 illustrate the extent to which Plodder Lane shed was responsible for the passenger train workings on the Bolton - Atherton -Tyldesley - Kenyon lines. Prior to World War 2, services in the latter area followed the pre-grouping pattern, with both the Bolton - Tyldesley-Leigh - Kenyon Jn. and the direct Bolton- Atherton - Kenyon Jn., trains consisting almost exclusively of two coach push-pull sets. In June, 1939 the service consisted of 10 trains each way between Bolton and Kenyon via Tyldesley, and a further 22 taking the direct route to Kenyon Jn. via West Leigh, several of which ran to and from Warrington or Liverpool. Included in the Kenyon line total were the summer long distance services to Chester and Llandudno, introduced by the LM&SR during the 1930's. For many years, these trains ran to close the following times, the details below being from the 1938 timetable:

		SX	SO
Bolton Gt. Moor St.	Dep.	10.05	12.55
Rumworth & Daubhill		10.09	13.00
Chequerbent		10.13	13.05
Atherton Bag Lane		10.19	13.10
West Leigh		10.25	13.17
Pennington		10.28	13.20
Kenyon Jn.		10.33	13.25
Llandudno	Arr.	13.10	
Chester	Arr.		14.21

In 1938, the return workings from Llandudno and Chester were scheduled to arrive in Bolton at 21.25 and 22.48, respectively. The Llandudno train is known to have been worked by Patricroft engines and crew, as the necessary light engine movements to and from that shed are shown in the working timetables for the period. However, it is believed that the Chester trains were worked by Plodder Lane men using Patricroft engines, usually a 'Precursor' 4-4-0.

During the early 1940's there was a good compliment of staff at Bolton Great Moor St., comprising a station master, station master's clerk, two platform foremen, three passenger guards, three call boys and one passenger shunter. As many of the trains that used Gt. Moor St. station were push-and-pull worked, the latter had to deal only with those that were not, and the run-around method for the latter trains is worthy of comment. The engine having arrived with its train in tow would set the coaches back through the crossover into the departure platform, then use the crossover to return to the arrival platform road. The coaches were then run by gravity down to the buffer stops of the departure platform, whereupon the engine used the crossover and then backed down onto the stock ready for the return working. When more extensive shunting was need, the maximum number of vehicles allowed to be shunted onto the station ramp was nine, provided that a brake vehicle was at the opposite end of the rake to the locomotive. In the absence of a brake vehicle, only three carriages could be shunted onto the station ramp beyond No. 1 signal box. Nine bogie vehicles was also the maximum number allowed for one locomotive in the entire Roe Green Jn. - Bolton - Atherton section. Within that limit the passenger train loadings, expressed simply in tons, were subject to the maxima specified in Table 11:

Table 11. Working of Passenger Trains by Passenger and Freight Engines

From	To	Direction	Class of Engine									
			Passenger						Freight			
			1	2	3	4	5	5X	2	3	4	5
Pennington	Bolton	Up*	75	105	125	140	160	180	115	135	150	175
		Down	125	170	205	230	265	300	185	225	250	290
Bolton	Roe Green Jn	Either	125	170	205	230	265	300	185	225	250	290

*When assisted in rear from Atherton to Chequerbent or Hulton Sidings, the following loads may be conveyed:

Class of Engine	2	3	4	5	5X
Tons	150	170	220	240	260

Engines were allowed to assist passenger trains from Atherton to Chequerbent only by banking at the rear of the train.

Train services throughout the period under discussion had been maintained at pre-first world war levels. The 1910 timetable, for example, had 34(SX) and 36(SO) departures from Bolton Gt. Moor St., of which 19 were for the Kenyon line, 10(SX) and 11(SO) for Manchester, and the remainder for Monton Green. The services were reorganised in Autumn 1935, one result of which was a slight increase in the number of trains so that by 1937 the timetable listed 44(SX) and 52(SO) departures from Bolton, with motor trains running to Tyldesley, Kenyon Jn., Newton, Earlestown, and St. Helens, in addition to services on the Manchester route. However, restrictions during the second world war did not deal kindly with the passenger services from Bolton Gt. Moor St. The Bolton -Tyldesley-Leigh push and pull service was withdrawn in 1942, and the remaining services on the Kenyon line cut back so that by 1947 there were only eight weekday trains each way between Bolton and Kenyon Jn, with an additional train on Saturdays. The service was now entirely a local one; all trains stopped at every station along the route. On the Little Hulton line the changes were less extensive, being confined to a reduction in the number of trains. In November 1947 there were only 5 through trains from Bolton Gt. Moor St. to Manchester Exchange on weekdays, with two additional Saturday trains, the service being supplemented by three trains that ran from Bolton only as far as Monton Green. In the down direction through service was also provided by five trains daily, with two additional Saturday trains. This was in stark contrast to the June 1939 timetable, which listed 20 trains through trains each way between Bolton and Manchester, but the changes were not surprising: the former L&YR route from Bolton Trinity St. to Manchester Victoria offered an intensive service, with trains running approximately every 15 minutes throughout the day in the 1930's and 1940's, and included frequent Sunday trains. Typical journey times from Trinity St. station to Manchester were 18 minutes for non-stop trains and 28 minutes for stopping trains, compared with the 35-40 minutes taken by all trains on the Gt. Moor St. line. The conclusions were inevitable: the former L&NWR route could not compete for through traffic between Bolton and Manchester. Its role in serving intermediate stations, which was also the principal *raison d'etre* for the passenger trains from Bolton to Leigh and Kenyon, had been seriously undermined by the development of the local road transportation network, and the final outcome, for passenger trains at least, was inevitable.

FREIGHT WORKINGS IN THE BR ERA, 1948-1954

Although some reduction in goods services relative to pre-war years was experienced, mineral traffic during this period was not subject to the same level of decline. Levels during the war were high, and even into the early 1950's a substantial amount of traffic was handled at Crook St. yard. Table 12 lists the freight trains and associated light engine movements at Plodder Lane during the summer of 1952, and illustrates the extent to which the mineral traffic in particular had been maintained, at least on weekdays. Of special note is the Liverpool (Edge Hill) connection, and that a Warrington to Bolton train was now scheduled to run via Monton Green and Plodder Lane. The latter practice began during the late 1940's when the Atherton - Bolton route was closed at night, at which time two trains nightly from Warrington reached Bolton via Roe Green. A light engine from Plodder Lane was sent to Roe Green to collect the first train from Warrington, which would then be banked by the Warrington - Roe Green train engine as far as Plodder Lane. The latter locomotive then returned light engine to Roe Green to collect the second train from Warrington, but by 1952 only one such working appeared in the timetables. Local traffic to Highfield Sidings and Little Hulton Jn. was still heavy, but Walkden Sidings was not extensively used, with only one train daily to Plodder Lane. All trains were class K (mineral) with the exception of the 22.02 Bolton to Liverpool Road, designated as class H goods.

Plate 70. Adelaide St. Bolton, about 1950. The original alignment of the Bolton & Leigh Railway had crossed Adelaide St. by a low overbridge which, after the deviation route opened in 1885, became the end of Daubhill coal sidings Photo, J.Jones.

Table 12. Freight Traffic at Plodder Lane, Summer 1952

Train	From	Plodder Lane Arr	Plodder Lane Dep.	To	Notes
Light Engine	Bolton	Pass	03.12	Monton Green	MX. To collect Warrington train from loop
Class K	Ordsall Lane	04.18	04.33	Bolton	MX.
Class K	Warrington	04.46	04.48	Bolton	MX. Stops to change enginemen
Light Engine			15.15	Bolton	MX
Light Engine			05.30	Bolton	MO
Class K	Ordsall Lane	05.27	05.49	Bolton	MO
Light Engine			06.20	Bolton	MX
Class K	Bolton	06.45			MX
LE+Van			07.10	Bolton	
Class K	Bolton	pass	08.40	Little Hulton Jn.	Spends 40 mins at Lever St.
Class K	Little Hulton Jn.	09.20	09.45	Bolton	MX
Class K	Bolton	10.20			MO
Class K	Bolton	10.55			MX
Class K			11.15	Little Hulton Jn.	SO. Shunts Highfield Sidings 11.09-11.40
Light Engine+Van			11.15	Little Hulton Jn.	SX
Light Engine	Bolton	11.28			
Class K	Walkden Sidings	11.55			
Class K			12.25	Little Hulton Jn.	SX. Shunts Highfield Sidings 12.20-13.15
Light Engine	Leigh	12.35			Via Roe Green
Light Engine	Edge Hill	12.45			Via Bolton after working from Atherton.
Light Engine			12.58	Atherton	
Light Engine	Walkden Sidings	13.00			SO
Light Engine			13.40	Bolton	
Empties	Little Hulton Jn.	13.46	13.50	Bolton	SX
Light Engine	Atherton	14.05			MSX. Via Bolton

Train	From	Plodder Lane Arr	Dept	To	Notes
Class K	Patricroft	pass	14.06	Bolton	SX
Light Engine			14.33	Atherton	SX
Light Engine			14.33	Chanters Sidings	SO
Class K	Bolton	pass	14.45	Little Hulton Jn.	SX. Shunts Highfield Sidings when required.
Light Engine			15.30	Bolton	To work 15.45 to Chanters Sidings
Light Engine			15.45	Bolton	SO
Class K	Little Hulton Jn.	16.10			SX. Loco to shed.
Class K			16.40	Bolton	SX
Light Engine	Bolton	17.38			
Light Engine	Bolton	19.40			SO
Light Engine	Bolton	20.12			SX
Light Engine	Bolton	20.42			SX
Light Engine	Bolton	20.48			SX
Light Engine	Bolton	21.05			SO
Light Engine	Tyldesley	21.14			SX. Via Roe Green
Light Engine			21.35	Bolton	SX. To work 21.50 goods to Liverpool Road.
Class K	Jackson's Sidings	21.50	21.55	Bolton	SX
Class H	Bolton	22.02	22.07	Liverpool Road	SX
Light Engine	Bolton	22.12			After working 20.30 from Kenyon Jn.
Light Engine	Bolton	pass	22.50	Patricroft Shed	

PASSENGER TRAINS: THE FINAL DEVELOPMENTS, 1948-1954

Nationalisation of the railways in 1948 brought no respite in the reductions of trains services from Bolton Gt. Moor St. By the summer of 1950 there were only seven up and eight down trains daily between Kenyon Jn. and Bolton, a number of which ran through to Warrington, with three additional trains on Saturdays and one running only on Tuesdays and Thursdays (Bolton's market days). Services on the Manchester route in 1950 were substantially unchanged from those of 1947, but this was soon to change. By September 1953 the short trips from Bolton to Monton Green had been discontinued, and there were only four trains each way on weekdays between Bolton and Manchester. Kenyon line services had suffered similar losses, with only five daily trains remaining in the up direction (to Bolton) and six from Bolton to Kenyon Jn. On this route, both the local and long distance trains were affected, and only two of the remaining trains ran to and from Warrington; Rumworth & Daubhill and Chequerbent stations were closed in March 1952. The full passenger timetables for the services from Bolton Gt. Moor St. are reproduced in Tables 13 - 16. Tables 13 and 14 make an interesting comparison with the opening services between Bolton and Manchester of 1875. The basic pattern of trains is essentially the same, comprising early morning trains in each direction, a gap during the mid-morning and mid-afternoons, a late night service (now Saturdays only), and, of course, no Sunday trains.

Plate 71 (Right) Although the section from Atherton Jn. to Pennington South Jn. had closed on 17th. June 1963, Class 8F 2-8-0 No.48663, prepares to leave Atherton Bag for Kenyon Jn. with an LCGB brake van special on 15th. July of that year as, in *Plate 72* below, participants of the excursion gather in the goods yard.

Photo, Author.

Plate 72 (Left) The passenger station is visible to the left of the locomotive's tender, with the signal box on the down platform and at the end of the up platform the milepost '5' and gradient post are evident, the latter proclaiming a moderate 1 in 322 through the immediate station area before the climb to Chequerbent began in earnest.

Photo, J.Marshall.

Table 13. Passenger Trains, Manchester Exchange to Bolton, Weekdays only, September 1953

	SX			SO	SX	SO
Manchester Ex.	06.33	07.32	08.10	12.15	17.25	20.50
Ordsall Lane	06.36	07.35		12.18	17.28	20.53
Cross Lane		07.38		12.21	17.31	20.56
Seedley		07.40		12.23	17.33	
Eccles		07.45	08.18	12.28	17.38	21.02
Monton Green	06.45	07.49	08.22	12.32	17.42	21.06
Worsley	06.48	07.52	08.25	12.35	17.45	21.09
Walkden L.L.		07.58	08.31	12.41	17.51	21.15
Little Hulton	06.55	08.02	08.35	12.46	17.55	21.20
Plodder Lane	07.00	08.07	08.40	12.51	18.02	21.25
Bolton Gt. Moor St.	07.06	08.13	08.46	12.57	18.08	21.31

Table 14. Passenger Trains, Bolton to Manchester Exchange, Weekdays only, September 1953

				SO	SX	SO
Bolton Gt. Moor St.	06.30	07.25	08.09	13.20	17.45	23.00
Plodder Lane	06.35	07.30	08.14	13.25	17.51	23.05
Little Hulton	06.39	07.34	08.18	13.29	17.55	23.09
Walkden L.L.	06.42	07.37	08.21	13.32	17.58	23.12
Worsley	06.46	07.41	08.25	13.36	18.02	23.16
Monton Green	06.49	07.44	08.29	13.39	18.05	23.19
Eccles	06.53	07.48	08.34	13.43.	18.10	23.23
Seedley	06.57	07.52	08.38	13.47	18.14	
Cross Lane	07.00	07.55	08.41	13.49	18.16	
Ordsall Lane	07.04	07.59	08.45	13.52	18.20	
Manchester Ex.	07.10	08.05	08.50	13.57	18.25	23.33

Plate 73. On 27th. March 1954, passengers pose for the cameraman as the last passenger train on the Bolton-Kenyon route calls at Westleigh station.

Photo, D.Hill collection.

Table 15. Passenger Trains, Kenyon to Bolton, Weekdays only, September 1953

			SO	TThSO			SX	SO	SO
Warrington Bank Quay	06.15					17.00			
Earlestown	06.24					17.08			
Newton-Le-Willows	06.27					17.11			
Kenyon Jn.	06.42	08.03	12.40	13.22	16.29	17.25	17.58	19.15	21.45
Pennington	06.44	08.05	12.42	13.24	16.32	17.27	18.00	19.18	21.47
West Leigh	06.50	08.08	12.45	13.27	16.34	17.30	18.03	19.21	21.50
Atherleigh	06.54	08.11	12.48	13.30	16.37	17.33	18.06	19.24	21.53
Atherton Bag Lane	06.59	08.16	12.53	13.35	16.42	17.38	18.11	19.29	21.58
Bolton Gt. Moor St.	07.12	08.29	13.16	13.48	16.55	17.31	18.24	19.42	22.11

Table 16. Passenger Trains, Bolton to Kenyon, Weekdays only, September 1953

	SX			SO	SO	TThO				SO
Bolton Gt. Moor St.	06.49	07.20	08.23	12.00	13.50	15.35	16.23	17.05	18.03	22.35
Atherton Bag Lane	06.59	07.30	08.35	12.10	14.00	15.45	16.33	17.15	18.13	22.45
Atherleigh	07.02	07.33	08.38	12.13	14.03	15.48	16.36	17.18	18.16	22.48
West Leigh	07.05	07.36	08.41	12.16	14.06	15.51	16.39	17.21	18.19	22.51
Pennington	07.08	07.39	08.44	12.19	14.09	15.54	16.42	17.24	18.22	22.54
Kenyon Jn.	07.12	07.44	08.49	12.24	14.12	15.59	16.47	17.29	18.27	22.59
Newton-Le-Willows	07.18		08.57							
Earlestown	07.21		09.00							
Warrington Bank Q.	07.30		09.13							

Ironically, concurrent with the reduction in services the variety of locomotives working from Bolton Gt. Moor St. station was perhaps greater at this period than at any other. This was a result of locomotive transfers and flexible rostering; Patricroft shed had always provided locomotives for a good proportion of passenger trains on the Manchester and Bolton route, but now Sutton Oak (St. Helens) and Warrington locomotives appeared regularly in Bolton. On the Kenyon route this brought in the then new Class 4, 2-6-0 tender engines of the 43XXX series, Class 2, 2-6-2T's such as Nos.40080, 40084 and 40108 from Sutton Oak, and Class 4, 2-6-4T's Nos.42606 and 42607 from Warrington, while on the Manchester line the Fowler LM&SR 2-6-2T's were not uncommon. A remarkable development was the regular rostering of a Class 5, 4-6-0, and occasionally a 'Jubilee' 4-6-0, on the 17.25 SX Manchester Exchange to Bolton. This was obviously a 'fill-in' turn between main line duties, and is recorded on one occasion as being hauled by No.45563 *Australia*. The locomotive from this train did not return directly to Manchester: it was initially scheduled to run as light engine from Bolton via Howe Bridge West Jn. to Wigan, but by 1951 was utilised for working a freight train from Bolton to Atherton. Prior to this time, these engines had only rarely been seen at Plodder Lane. A Warrington engine worked the first train of the day into Bolton Gt. Moor St. from the Atherton direction, the 06.15 from Warrington Bank Quay, which was rarely on time during the winter months as it usually needed assistance to surmount Chequerbent incline on the damp and sometimes icy rails.

The story of the closure battles is told in Chapter 6; suffice it to say here that closure took place from 29th. March 1954, but as there were no Sunday trains the last regular passenger trains from Bolton Gt. Moor St. to both Manchester and Kenyon Jn. ran on the previous Saturday, March 27th. As usual with such events, matters concerning the last trains were recorded in detail. On the Kenyon line, the 2-coach

22.35 left from Platform 1 at Gt. Moor St. behind BR Class 2, 2-6-2T No.84003, which had worked most of the services on the line during that day; a short time later, the final regular passenger train from Bolton Gt. Moor St., the 3-coach 23.00 to Manchester, left behind 2-6-4T No.42574. This was a Patricroft engine and had previously worked the last train from Manchester to Bolton. After arriving in Manchester with the last up train, the engine worked light back to Patricroft sheds. Ironically, 42574 was to remain loyal to the Bolton area, for it subsequently spent many years working from the ex. L&YR sheds on Crescent Road.

Plate 74. (Left) Driver J. Bethel of Patricroft, in charge of 2-6-4T No.42574, greets passengers for the last regular passenger train from Bolton Gt. Moor St., the 23.00 Saturdays only to Manchester exchange, on 27th. March 1954. The fireman on this occasion was A.J. McClane, also from Patricroft.

Photo, Tillotsons Ltd.

Plate 75. (Below) Class 8F 2-8-0 No.48663 at Pennington South Jn. on 15th. July 1963, returning to Atherton Bag Lane with an LCGB brake van special. The junction of the lines from Leigh (above the train) and Plank Lane (from the right) was located underneath the bridge in the background, just north of which was Pennington South Jn. signal box. The box remained open until 14th. March 1966 to serve trains from the Tyldesley and Leigh directions.

Photo, Author.

SPECIAL TRAINS, 1954 - 1964

Although Bolton Gt. Moor St. station was used by excursion trains prior to 1954, details of these have proved somewhat scarce. A popular pre-war excursion from Gt. Moor St. and Plodder Lane was a Saturday evening trip to Belle Vue (Manchester). These trains ran via Castlefield Jn. to Longsight station, from where a covered walkway led to the Gardens at Belle Vue. The return journey left Longsight around midnight, and if delayed could arrive at Plodder Lane as late as 02.00. Also during the 1920's and 1930's an excursion train was run during the summer to take the orphans of the Hollin's Cottage Homes from Plodder Lane to Hoylake, where they spent two weeks under canvas. One such trip employed 'Precursor' 4-4-0 No.5223 *Snake*, working tender-first to Bolton, where it would run round before taking the Atherton direction for its final destination.

It is known that during the early 1950's half day and evening excursions to Blackpool and Southport were run via Atherton, Howe Bridge West Junction and Wigan, usually using a Class 4F 0-6-0 as motive power (although other engines such as the L&YR 0-6-0's and LM&SR Class 5 4-6-0's were recorded). On one occasion in 1950, Plodder Lane Class 4F 0-6-0 No.44473 worked an excursion from Bolton Gt. Moor St. to Southport via Leigh and Wigan. The closure battles discussed below shed some light on excursion traffic at this relatively late date in the line's history, recording trains to Belle Vue and football excursion traffic in late 1953/early 1954.

Following closure in 1954, Bolton Gt. Moor St. station continued to be opened on an annual basis during the town's holiday weeks in June/July for North Wales excursion traffic. The booking office at Gt. Moor St. station was opened for excursion ticket sales a week before the holidays started, with staff temporarily transferred from Trinity Street station. On holiday weekends a locomotive, often an ex. L&NWR 0-8-0, was sent from Patricroft sheds to shunt the empty stock for the excursion trains, a task made more difficult after July 1956 when the up (southbound) line on the ramp to the passenger station removed, and by the removal of the signal arms from the posts in Gt. Moor St. station and along the ramp to Fletcher St.. This excursion traffic continued until 1958, when during the last full weekend of excursions almost 2800 passengers used the following trains from Bolton Gt. Moor St. on Saturday 28th. June:

Departure	Destination
06.25	Prestatyn and stations to Bangor
07.00	Prestatyn and stations to Llandudno
07.38	Ditto
08.00	Afonwen and Penychain (Butlins)
09.24	Bangor, Caernarvon, Afonwen and Penychain
11.55	Prestatyn and Rhyl
12.14	Prestatyn and stations to Llandudno
12.44	Ditto
13.30	Ditto

The last excursion train to depart from Gt. Moor St. for North Wales was a day excursion, the 09.30 to Llandudno, on 9th. July 1958. Three days later, the last to arrive reached the station from North Wales at 17.18. Motive power for the North Wales excursions was provided from Patricroft sheds, and usually consisted of LM&SR or BR Class 5 4-6-0's, although the use of 2-6-0 and even Class 4F 0-6-0 engines was not unknown, and Patricroft provided all the footplate staff. From 1959, the North Wales excursions were handled exclusively by Trinity St. station in Bolton.

Although Bolton Gt. Moor St. had seen its last regular excursion train in 1958, the lines in the area were to carry others in subsequent years, for enthusiast's excursion trains, growing in popularity in the late 1950's and 1960's, were to visit the area on several occasions. The first, operated by the Railway Correspondence and Travel Society in July 1953 used ex. L&YR 2-4-2T No.50644 to cover the Howe Bridge West Jn - Bolton - Roe Green section among other routes in South Lancashire. On 4th. April 1959, the same Society's 'South Lancashire Freight Lines Railtour' used 2-6-4T No.42289 to visit the ex L&NWR lines in the Bolton area.

Closure of the section from Atherton Jn. to Pennington South Jn. was commemorated by the Locomotive Club of Great Britain (LCGB) on 15th June 1963, when Class 8F 2-8-0 No.48663 hauled a special train of six brake vans from Atherton Bag Yard goods yard to Kenyon Jn. and back. On the return journey, the train stopped just north of Pennington South Jn. to allow participants to explore the remains of the flyover that once gave trains from the Wigan direction direct access to the Leigh line. The LCGB was also responsible for the

next special to visit the area, the 'South Lancashire Limited' railtour of 21st. September . 1963. This train of six passenger coaches left Liverpool Road station in Manchester behind Class 8F 2-8-0 No.48178 and ran via Roe Green and Howe Bridge East to Bolton, where it stopped on the ramp to Gt. Moor St. station with the locomotive only yards from Bolton No. 1 signal box. The train was then taken via Fletcher St. and Plodder Lane to Little Hulton Jn. by 3F 0-6-0T No.47378, where it ran onto the branch in order for the locomotive to run round and return the train to Bolton. At Bolton, 47378 was replaced by 48178 for the run to Wigan (Central) via Howe Bridge West Jn. and Hindley South. On reversal at Wigan, the train ran back to Hindley and then at Bickershaw Jn. took the direct line to Pennington and on to Kenyon Jn. before joining the Liverpool line, later heading north again at Parkside Jn. for Horwich, a tour of the works, and the remainder of the 102 mile railtour that concluded in Manchester Central. The timings for this train on the Howe Bridge East - Bolton - Little Hulton - Bolton - Howe Bridge West section are summarised in Table 17.

Plate 76. It is Bolton holiday weekend, 29th. June 1957, and L&NWR 0-8-0 No.49027 has been sent from Patricroft to act as station pilot for the excursion trains from Bolton Gt. Moor St. The engine is ready to move an empty stock train from the siding east of the passenger ramp (the truncated original route of the Bolton and Leigh line), down to Fletcher St. and then up the ramp into the passenger station. The photograph was taken from the ramp to the station, the ramp being visible to the extreme right. In the background is the imposing bulk of the Bridgeman St. goods warehouse, while immediately behind the tender two wagons can be seen standing in Hulton's Coal yard sidings.

Photo, C.B.Golding.

Table 17. Timings of the LCGB 'South Lancashire Limited':, 21st. September 1963.

Howe Bridge - Bolton: Class 8F 2-8-0 No.48178 + 6 coaches
Bolton - Little Hulton Jn.: Class 3F 0-6-0T No.47378 + 6 coaches

		Sched.	Actual
Howe Bridge East Jn.	pass	09.56	09.59½
Atherton Jn.	pass	09.58	10.00¼
Atherton Bag Lane	arr.		10.03
	dep.		10.04
Summit of incline	pass		10.13
Chequerbent	pass		10.14
Rumworth & Daubhill	pass		10.15
Fletcher St. Jn.	pass		10.19½
Crook St. (Bolton)	arr.	10.10	10.21½
	dep.	10.20	10.34
Lever St.	arr.		10.36/10.47
	dep.		10.45/10.52
Plodder Lane	arr.		10.56
	dep.		10.59
Little Hulton Jn.	arr.	10.32	11.02
	dep.	10.50	11.13
Plodder Lane	pass		11.22
Lever St.	arr.		11.26
	dep.		11.28
Crook St. (Bolton)	arr.	11.02	11.32
	dep.	11.10	11.41
Fletcher St. Jn.	pass		11.44
Rumworth & Daubhill	pass		11.48½
Chequerbent	pass		11.52½
Atherton Bag Lane	pass		11.58
Atherton Jn.	pass	11.23	11.59½
Howe Bridge West Jn.	pass	11.29	12.00½

Much of the time lost on this section of the tour was attributable to the Chequerbent incline and to unscheduled halts at Lever St. (twice) and Plodder Lane, the Lever St. manoeuvres being to pick up a pilotman with keys to unlock the Little Hulton Jn. ground frame. No. 48178 took the train unaided up the Chequerbent incline, passing the summit at an estimated 20 mph in 9 minutes from a standing start at Atherton Bag Lane.   Later in the day, when returning from Wigan to Pennington, this train had the distinction of covering some of the most decrepit track ever used by passenger stock; some of it was underwater, and in places the fireman had to walk ahead of the locomotive to remove household debris such as discarded bicycles and washing machines from the tracks.

Less than one year after this railtour, the LCGB was once again active in the Bolton area when, on 9th. May 1964, a brakevan special was organised for several short trips in the Crook St. area. No. 47378 was again used, this time for the remaining section of the High Street line as far as Magee, Marshall's sidings, and for a trip to the Dawes St. coal drops adjacent to Gt. Moor St. station. In addition, Class. 8F No.48770 took the tour to Little Hulton Jn. as part of the scheduled freight service for that day.

Chapter 5.

Running the Railway at Plodder Lane.

In the early 1940's there were five gangs of cleaners totalling 22 men at Plodder Lane, booking on at 00.01, 06.00, 09.00, and 12.00 every day except Sundays, and 21.00 Monday - Thursday, 18.00 Friday and 14.30 Saturday, finishing at 23.00 on Saturday as Plodder Lane was closed from 06.00 until midnight on Sundays. Regular cleaning turns were six 8-hour days with a 30 minute meal break allowance daily, giving a working week of 48 hrs. At this time there was very little cleaning done, as most of the cleaners were passed as firemen and were out on the road, while the others were employed on labouring jobs around the shed such as coal stacking until, later in the war, coal became so scarce that the stack was empty and any new coal was used immediately on arrival. As Plodder Lane was closed on Sundays there were no Sunday duties, but during times of staff shortages elsewhere Plodder Lane passed cleaners and firemen were often 'lent out' for Sunday turns at Springs Branch or Patricroft.

In addition to the cleaners, there two shed turners, both drivers whose eyesight had deteriorated such that they could no longer work on the main line and whose job it now was to move engines around the shed. As engines came on shed, they were left on the disposal pit where the fire was cleaned or dropped, according to whether the engine was to be used again shortly or was to be stabled in the shed for boiler washing or repairs, and the ashpan and smokebox were emptied. These jobs were done by a shed labourer, after which the shed turner took the engine under the coaling stage where it was coaled by hand and the tank or tender filled. It was a peculiarity of Plodder Lane that no locomotive water was available at the shed building, so engines were filled at the coaling stage and stabled with full tanks. Between fire cleaning and coaling, the engine would be turned if required. After coaling the engine was stabled in the shed, and the turner was responsible for placing engines on the correct road and in the right order so that they could leave in turn the following morning. One shed turner booked on a 08.00 and the other at 22.00. The day man also shunted out empty coal wagons from the coaling stage ramp and replaced them with full ones.

The next link in order of seniority also had two jobs. This was the Crook St. shunt, usually at this period with 0-6-0T No.7401. The morning turn booked on at 06.00, prepared the engine and then ran light to Crook St. yard for a very busy day. The afternoon men booked on at 13.30, and shortly thereafter the engine would arrive back at the shed for relief and re-coaling (water could be taken at Crook St.), going back to work at Crook St. until about 21.00 when it returned to the shed for the night.

The next link up was the goods link, whose jobs in the early 1940's were:

Plate 77 , (opposite) A view of Crook St. yard from Fletcher St. bridge on 20th. March 1963. The sidings on the extreme right lead past the Bridgeman St. goods warehouse, while the next siding over, alongside the ramp to the passenger station, leads to the Wm. Hulton coal yard and the Hick, Hargreaves Soho foundry sidings. By this period, only a single line of rails ran up the ramp to passenger station. An unidentified Class 8F 2-8-0 is in Crook St. yard, and behind the locomotive is the 1874 goods warehouse. The water tank is in the centre of the photograph, and to its left is the cattle dock, behind which is the rear of the Bolton Corporation bus garage, with the door in the end wall allowing rail access to the building. The 0-6-0T locomotive, No.47378, is sitting on the road which leads to the Co-operative Wholesale Society's coalyard, and the Manchester (formerly Bridgewater) Collieries sidings. The notice board by the engine reads 'Engines must not pass this board on the left hand side of the road'. Presumably, shunting engines were immune to this restriction!

Photo, E.F.Bentley collection.

01.50 Bolton to Bamfurlong, trip working

03.30 Bolton to Daubhill, shunting and trip working

04.15 Atherton to Edge Hill (Liverpool) and return

04.30 bank engine relief

06.05 Bolton to Walkden and Plodder Lane sidings, trip working

07.50 Cushions to Warrington, then work 10.02 Froghall to Manchester Ship Canal Sidings (Warrington engine)

10.10 Bolton to Wigan and return (via Parkside and Kenyon) (the 'day Wigan')

11.00 Lever St. and Bolton shunting and trip working

13.20 Coal empties, Bolton to Westleigh and Kenyon and return (trip 81)

13.30 Coal empties, Bolton to Chanter's Colliery (shunt), return coal working to Bolton (trip 82)

13.40 Bolton to Walkden and Little Hulton, trip working

15.10 Coal empties, Bolton to Tyldesley, Kenyon and return to Bolton (the 'Fiddler')

16.00 Atherton bank engine

18.05 Bolton to Warrington (Arpley)

19.05 Bolton to Warrington (Froghall) and return (through freight)

20.30 bank engine relief

21.35 Bolton to Ordsall Lane and return (through freight)

Several of the above duties were given nicknames. It is noteworthy that, in spite of the reduction in trip workings at this relatively late date, Crook St. yard was still shunted from early morning to late evening, and a bank engine was provided at Atherton throughout the day. The method of trip working in the above freight train rosters is worthy of comment. In L&NWR days men were paid for each 'trip', so that if a trip should take, for example, two hours and it could be completed in 90 minutes, the men were still paid for two hours work and could start the next trip immediately. This acted as a positive incentive, and explains in part the image of L&NWR engines being flogged unmercifully to keep trains moving. This trip payment system was abolished by the LM&SR, but many former L&NWR men still worked to the old pattern when rostered for L&NWR engines. The LMS Class 4F 0-6-0's were found not to be so amenable to the same treatment!

One up from the goods link was the motor link. These were all push-and-pull workings, and as this required the fireman to be in sole charge of the locomotive these jobs were not rostered for the passed cleaners, but only for the registered firemen. At this time, turns in the motor link at Plodder began by working the following trains:

06.18 Tyldesley, Wigan North Western and return

06.45 Warrington, then to Wigan North Western, returning to Warrington for the 13.11 to Bolton

07.28 Kenyon and return at 08.10

12.15 Monton Green and return at 13.20

13.50 Newton-Le-Willows and return at 16.21

16.20 Kenyon and return at 17.27

16.25 Monton Green and return at 16.50

17.05 to Kenyon, then 17.45 to Tyldesley

17.25 Monton Green, returning at 18.40

22.35 Kenyon and return with empty stock

The top link had four jobs and was referred to by Plodder Lane men as the 'steam link'. All the trains in this link were non push-and-pull, and so could be worked by passed cleaners. The initial jobs covered by this link were:

06.05 Leigh and Manchester Exchange, returning to Bolton at 07.32
06.30 Manchester Exchange, returning at 08.10
07.25 Manchester Exchange, returning at 12.07 (Saturdays Only)
17.45 Manchester, then empty stock working from Ordsall Lane to Manchester Exchange

Each locomotive in the passenger links was allocated two separate crews for morning and afternoon workings. The top-link drivers, verging on retirement, were C. Beamish, H. Collier, G. Longworth, and J.R. Parton, with other drivers A. Barnett, G. Bibby, J. Donnelly, J. Glover, G. Hampson, J. Holmes, and W. Jones, and firemen R. Collier, B. Cooper, G. Glover, G. Monogan, J. Ritson, H. Scowcroft, G. Smith, and S. Worrell.

Plate 78. On the footplate of a L&NWR 0-8-0, Plodder Lane passed fireman Bob Hindle is seen on the left, with the driver leaning against the cab rails. The photograph is undated, but presumably taken during wartime as the blackout tarpaulin can be seen hanging from the cab roof.

Photo. Maureen Mitchell.

Work at Plodder Lane alternated between periods of furious activity and relative calm. On a typical day a steady flow of work started from midnight. The night foreman, Jack Rainford during the early 1940's, would have arrived at 23.00 and the 21.00 cleaning shift would still be on duty as the midnight cleaners arrived. No outside cleaning was done on night turns, but emphasis was placed on the big ends, eccentrics and valve gear of the passenger tanks that had to be ready for the drivers to oil them before the early morning turns could leave the shed. Access to the inside motion of the tanks was not too difficult for a young cleaner, but as it involved squeezing into a small space between the firebox and the big ends by climbing up the pit walls from underneath the engine, was an awkward task for a senior driver to achieve, resulting in unofficial arrangements whereby the cleaners actually oiled these parts whilst cleaning them.

An important component of night work at the shed were the duties performed by the 'Knocker Ups', two of whom arrived to start work at midnight. One, usually Albert Whitehead, took charge of the Farnworth area south of the shed while the other, Jerry Marsden, was responsible for the Bolton side. Non-railway 'Knocker-Ups' who had to wake millworkers had a relatively easy task; they would start at around 05.00 and work their way down a street with a pole to knock on the bedroom windows of those on early shift. Railway work was different, however, in that men were required to book on all night at irregular intervals, and as driver and fireman often lived in different parts of the town, 'knocking-up' could involve covering great distances, often returning to the same area several times during the night, all done on foot, without a watch, usually without a torch, and in the early years of the war carried out under blackout conditions. As it was impossible for the 'Knocker-Up' to be in two places simultaneously, the official hour's notice prior to booking-on time was rendered flexible by agreement between the parties involved. If the regular 'Knocker-Up' was sick or on holiday, the replacement was a junior member of the cleaning staff, resulting in 16 or 17 year old youths wandering the streets alone all night, often lost in the blackout conditions. It was during these conditions that Leslie Cadman, then 16 years old, was on 'Knocking-Up' duties one night. On returning to the shed at 03.30 for a meal break, he was walking down the 'ginnell' to the shed when he encountered something that caused him to run furiously into the mess room in a state of panic, convinced that he had seen a ghost, which he described as a strange white shape, uttering alarming sounds and clanking a chain. Of course he was not believed, and when it came time to resume duties he was reluctant to venture out alone, but as no-one took him seriously he had no option but to return to work. Several minutes later, however, he was back in the mess room with the 'ghost' behind him, a large white goat that had escaped its tether and had been wandering around outside the shed with a long chain attached to its collar! The goat made itself comfortable by the mess room fire for the rest of the night, and was handed over to the police the following morning.

Continuing with the night's activities at Plodder Lane, the first locomen to arrive started at 01.50. Their engine had been prepared, and they left at 02.05 for Crook St. The usual work on this turn involved taking 36 empty coal wagons to Atherton, returning to Hulton Sidings with 17 full wagons, then back to Atherton for another 17 wagons prior to bring all 34 loaded wagons to Crook St. as a single train. This trip was done three times during the shift.

The next crew to arrive booked on at 03.25 for the morning shunting and trip working to Daubhill, a turn which involved crossing St. Helens Road at Daubhill on the way to shunt the sidings at Adelaide Street. This was an ungated crossing and the method of working required both the signalman from Rumworth & Daubhill and the train guard to show red lights to road traffic. The signalman had to switch his box out during this operation, but returned at once to open the station and become porter and booking clerk. When the shunting was complete, he had to close the station between trains, help the train back across St. Helens Road, reopen the signal box to send the train to Atherton, then close the box and re-open the station for passengers! There was little road traffic in the very early morning, but if the train was delayed in Bolton it might be as late as 10.00 when shunting at Adelaide St. took place, and the disruption of road traffic was not a trivial matter.

The next crew to arrive at Plodder Lane booked on at 04.15 for the Liverpool job, which started with a light engine trip to Atherton. This was one of the very few engines that was scheduled to run smokebox first down the Chequerbent incline, and great care had to taken to ensure that the boiler was

Plate 79. During the 1930's a group of Plodder Lane enginemen are seen on the footpath between the Conservative Club and the station, with the station entrance visible to the right above the wooden fence. On the extreme right is passed cleaner Bob Hindle, known at Plodder Lane as 'Red Bob' on account of his bright red hair.

Photo, Maureen Mitchell.

full before going over the top, as the water in the gauge glass dropped alarmingly on the incline. No engines ever came up the bank tender first. This train carried mixed goods to Kenyon Jn., then made up a full load for Edge Hill, where the engine was turned, and worked a general goods train back to Wigan. A new train for Crook St was collected at Wigan, and on arrival at Bolton a light engine trip to Plodder Lane completed the working, often taking 10 - 12 hours from booking on, and regarded by the crew as a useful source of overtime.

Shortly after the Liverpool engine had left, the Chequerbent bank engine arrived at the shed for re-manning. At the same time, the morning passenger train crews were booking on as time was needed for the locomotives to collect their trains, position them at Great Moor St., and (during the winter months) provide at least 30 minutes for the steam heating to warm the carriages.

With the departure of the Crook St. shunting engine at 06.30 activity in the shed subsided somewhat. A set of men booked on at 07.45 to travel to Warrington for the 10.02 from Froghall to the Manchester Ship Canal Sidings at Eccles, stopping at Kenyon Jn. to drop off and collect traffic. The Warrington locomotive was then worked as a light engine back to Plodder Lane, and stayed on shed until around 18.00 when it was collected by a Warrington crew (who came in as passengers) for a return working from Crook St. to Warrington. This was one turn that provided a break from the monotony of Class 4F 0-6-0's and L&NWR 0-8-0's for Plodder Lane freight crews, as the engines provided by Warrington were varied, examples including Class 5 4-6-0's, 'Jubilee' 4-6-0's, WD 2-8-0's and even the USA 2-8-0's. During wartime it was not unknown for no engine to be available at Warrington, in which case the Plodder Lane men travelled back home as passengers, but on two consecutive occasions when no locomotive was provided at Warrington, Driver Harold Ewell and Passed Cleaner Jim Jones were sent back with an L&YR 2-4-2T as light engine to Horwich Loco Works for repair, returning to Bolton by tram from Horwich. On these occasions a pilot had to be provided from Wigan to Horwich, as men from the L&NWR side at Bolton had no experience of working over the former L&YR lines, and the arrival of a Plodder Lane crew in the former L&YR stronghold at Horwich was regarded as something of a seven-day wonder that such 'foreign' footplate men could handle 'their' engines. At this time Plodder Lane men had experience with the L&YR 2-4-2 tanks, however, as Nos. 10643 and 10644 had been allocated there since the early 1940's. These engines were generally not well regarded at Plodder Lane, being more prone to slipping than the coal tanks, but were welcomed with open arms by Driver George Bibby, a former L&YR man who appropriated the better of the two, 10643, for his own use. They sometimes slipped to a standstill on the bank from Roe Green, and needed rear-end assistance on Chequerbent bank more frequently than did the coal tanks.

During the morning, Plodder Lane could take on a deserted appearance as all the engines, with the exception of those stopped for repair or boiler washout, were out at work. After 09.00 there would be only one engine in steam, a L&NWR 0-8-0 that would leave just after 10.00 for the 'day Wigan' working. This involved light engine working to Crook St. to collect a train, then shunting at Hulton Sidings, probably using the single line to Booth's steelworks to collect a fabricated steel Bailey Bridge section, and shunting at Atherton prior to working to Bamfurlong. The return to Bolton was via the main line to Golborne Jn., Parkside to Kenyon Jn., and more shunting at Hulton Sidings to finish at Crook St. with a light engine trip back to Plodder Lane.

After 10.30 there would be another rush, with frantic activity as the early morning engines returned for fire-cleaning, re-coaling and preparation for the afternoon shifts. Coaling at the former L&NWR sheds without mechanised apparatus was hard work, as the ramps were lower than those of the former L&YR sheds and the coal had to be lifted into the locomotives. Men working on the coal stage at the latter sheds were classed as labourers and paid a

Plate 80. A view from the ramp to the passenger station of Crook St. yard on 21st. September 1963, looking towards the yard entrance at Fletcher St. Two Class 8F 2-8-0's, No.48115 being closest to the camera, wait to leave with coal traffic. Between the locomotives the platform of the cattle dock can be seen, and behind it the brick-built shunter's and yard facilities building that was constructed in the mid 1950's to replace a collection of ageing wooden huts and carriage bodies in the same location. The coaching stock on the ramp belongs to the LCGB 'South Lancashire Ltd.' Railtour that visited Bolton on that date.

Photo, Author.

fixed hourly rate, but the at the former L&NWR sheds coal men were differentiated from shed labourers in that, although paid the same hourly rate, the coal men could also earn an extra bonus of sixpence per ton after having loaded 8½ tons, which was defined as a days work. Often 12 to 13 tons would be handled by one man in a single shift at Plodder Lane, generating an extra two shillings per day, which in the context of the wages of the period was not insubstantial. At Plodder Lane, fire-cleaning was done by shed labourers and coaling by the coal men (and both by cleaners if neither were available), unlike the situation at larger modernised sheds with mechanical equipment where this work could be carried out by footplate men no longer engaged on main line duties. During slack periods of the day, the fire-cleaner also had to load the ashes that had

been removed from locomotive ashpans and smokeboxes into a wagon for disposal.

Between 11.00 and 11.30 an engine went off shed to assist the Crook St. shunt engine and carry out the trip working to Lever St. This was followed by another lull in the activities until after 13.00. At 13.40 a mixed freight/passenger turn left, usually with a Class 4F 0-6-0, beginning with a trip to Walkden to collect a train of loco coal from the exchange sidings. This was left in Plodder Lane goods yard, to be transferred to the shed as required, and the crew transferred to a coal tank to go to Gt. Moor St. to work the 17.45 to Manchester and then the 20.20 return. The latter was a heavily loaded train, usually six coaches, and required an all-out effort on behalf of the coal tank to get from Roe Green Jn. to the Highfield Road bridge. Also around

13.30, the shed saw a spurt of activity, as the local collieries began to produce coal from the late morning onwards and their loading stages required a fresh supply of empty wagons. These were trip-worked to the Atherton area, and full wagons collected. As the loaded trains gradually filled the siding space at Atherton the Chequerbent bank engine was kept busy, and a replacement locomotive for this purpose left Plodder Lane at 16.00.

The next engine was booked off to work the 18.05 from Crook St. to Warrington, calling at Atherton and Kenyon Jn. before terminating at Arpley Sidings in Warrington. This involved using the main line at Winwick Jn. to reach Winwick Quay Sidings, and under wartime conditions long delays were often experienced here, as trains could be queued on the main line loops as far as Crewe. After sorting the train at Winwick, the turn terminated at Arpley Sidings, after which the engine was taken to Dallam shed for turning and returned light to Plodder Lane. The following turn was similar, with the engine 'off shed' at 19.20 to work to Winwick Quay, but then proceeding light to Dallam shed to turn before heading for Froghall Sidings where a train for Bolton was collected. The Warrington turns were long ones, often 13 or 14 hours under wartime conditions, but nevertheless regarded as 'plum jobs' because of the overtime involved.

From 20.00 onwards Plodder Lane became very busy once again as the passenger engines came back in rapid succession for the night. One of the shed turners, Bill Entwistle, had a very loud voice and could be heard from Plodder Lane itself expressing his opinions while trying to get the locomotives stabled for the night as quickly as possible, so that they could be examined by fitters before the next day's work.

The last turn of the day at Plodder Lane was rostered for a L&NWR 0-8-0. The crew booked on at 21.20, and left the shed at 21.35 for Crook St. to collect the 22.20 general freight for Manchester, working tender first and stopping at Patricroft for an hour or so of shunting, then on to Ordsall Lane. On the return journey the only stop was at the Manchester Ship Canal exchange sidings in Eccles, where a peculiar move took place. The entire train was backed down a steep bank, round a sharp bend under the main line and onto the MSC system.

This move had to be done with great care as visibility was very restricted, and the heavy train was in danger of running away had a coupling have broken. Once in the MSC complex, one of their locomotives added wagons to the end of the train, during which the Plodder Lane crew would build up their fire for the assault ahead. When ready, the 0-8-0 charged at the bank, often with the MSC

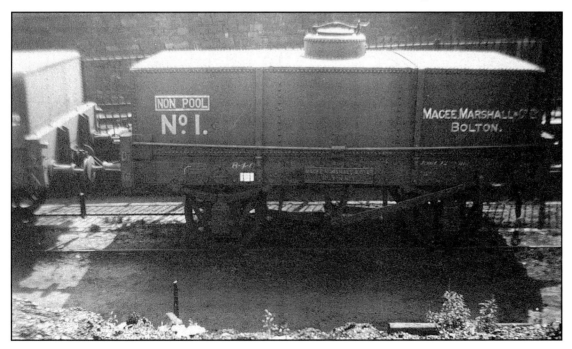

Plate 81. One of the tank wagons, No1, that was used to transport water from Burton-on-Trent is seen in the Magee, Marshall's siding in August 1956. The large rectangular cast iron plate in the centre of the solebar reads 'Magee, Marshall & Co. Ltd. Bolton No.1' The wagon was not fitted with the vacuum brake.

Photo, G.T.Hardy.

locomotive assisting (unofficially) at the rear, and it was heavy firing all the way to the Highfield Road bridge. Since this working was late at night and the signal boxes between Roe Green and Plodder Lane No. 2 were closed, the train could stop for a 'blow-up' if necessary without disrupting traffic, and certain drivers were known to take advantage of this to increase their overtime payments! In later years, this turn was expanded to include a Saturday working, but as the section from Roe Green was closed on Sundays the crew on this turn were booked to leave the engine at Patricroft and walk home along the track in the early hours of Sunday morning, five hours being allowed for the return trip.

Plate 82. (above) On 7th. December 1963, 3F 0-6-0T No. 47378, is shunting the yard at Crook St. Fletcher St. bridge is visible on the left hand side at the yard entrance. Just ahead of the locomotive are the remains of the cattle dock, with the locomotive servicing area, comprising a water tank, huts, and an ash dumping site, across from the shunter's cabin.   Photo, Author.

Plate 83.(left) At 6.45am on 22nd. July 1963, Class 8F 2-8-0 No.48178 pushes a row of wagons across St. Helens Road in Bolton. The locomotive is leaving the Daubhill coal yard and heading along the Bolton and Leigh route for the coal depot at Adelaide St., where it will shunt its train, deposit full coal wagons, and collect empties, before returning to Daubhill.   Photo, J.Marshall.

WORKING FROM PLODDER LANE

As a typical example of the work of the shed, consider a day in early September, 1941, when 3F 0-6-0T No.7401 was rostered, in the charge of driver Rupert Foster and passed cleaner Jim Jones, for the early morning trip working to Bolton, Plodder Lane and Walkden. On this occasion, there was no traffic for Walkden, but still a full day's work ahead. The crew booked on at 06.05 and took 7401 to Crook St. to collect a train that had previously been assembled. The first stop was back at Plodder Lane, where there was only one crossover road, close to No. 2 signal box, which meant that the train was left on the main line south of the crossover while the locomotive ran to Little Hulton Jn. to cross over, returning to Plodder Lane No. 2 on the down (Bolton) line, where it could now cross back to the up line and attach to the rear of its train in order to propel the train and shunt into Plodder Lane sidings from the north end. The traffic at this time was mainly full wagons of domestic coal for the yard, removal of any corresponding empties, and general merchandise for the goods shed, including a steady supply of Earle's cement in 1 cwt. bags for distribution to local building contractors. After an hour or so working the Plodder Lane yard, 7401 went to Little Hulton Jn. with coal and goods for Benniss' Foundry, whose private siding was located on the Little Hulton mineral line about 1/4 mile from the junction, where full wagons were positioned as required and empties plus loaded wagons picked up for movement to Crook St. The engine picked up the single line staff from Little Hulton Junction signal box and returned it on leaving the branch (the line was worked on the 'one engine in steam' principle) en route for Crook St. yard. Here, a new train was collected and taken to Lever St., which at this point in time handled only domestic and mill coal. Full wagons were positioned in Lever St. yard and the empties removed temporarily to Plodder Lane while the engine went into the shed yard to drop off loaded coal wagons and remove empties. By this time it was late morning, and with the

morning passenger trains out of the way the porter-signalman at Plodder Lane closed the station and opened No. 1 signal box at around 10.30 to enable shunting to take place from the southern end of the goods yard. Coal wagons were once again the main traffic, and as soon as the 12.20 Bolton to Manchester passenger train had cleared the line, 7401 set out for Highfield Sidings, the ground frame for which had been electrically released by the Plodder Lane porter-signalman from No. 1 signal box. The Scowcroft's coal depot at Highfield Sidings was not large, and was often congested, so that up to twenty or thirty wagons would often have to be left on the main line in order to allow shunting to take place. All of these had to be sorted and cleared before the next passenger train, the 13.30 to Manchester, left Bolton. By the time it reached Plodder Lane, 7401 and its train was on the Little Hulton branch at Little Hulton Jn., running round prior to heading for Crook St. for the third time that day. The method of running round at Little Hulton Jn. was unusual, and was dictated by the fact that there was only one crossover. As the main line to Manchester was downhill, the train was stopped ahead of the home signals and 7401 uncoupled and ran onto the branch. The engine then ran back towards Bolton until clear of the branch points, at which time the train brakes were released and the whole train, controlled by the guard in his van, was allowed to run onto the branch under gravity. Some further shunting was necessary to transfer the van to the rear (Manchester end) of the train, after which 7401 set off for Crook St. to deposit its load before returning to Plodder Lane for fire cleaning, coaling, and new set of train crew for the afternoon's work.

A trip on the Crook St. shunt engine meant leaving the shed around 06.30. After arriving in Crook St. yard the first job was often to sort wagons by using the old Bolton and Leigh line to High St as a headshunt. The procedure was for the engine (usually 0-6-0T 7401) to pull a raft of wagons up the hill towards High St. and stop on the incline. The wagon brakes were applied, and the engine dropped back a yard or so to ease the couplings, after which a shunter hooked off a few wagons at a time, which were allowed to run by gravity into the appropriate road in the Crook St. yard. This was a very dangerous practice, especially in frosty weather, as there would often be two or three rakes of wagons running down the hill at any one time. It was also a demanding procedure, especially when shunting with a 'special tank' 0-6-0ST, known locally as 'humpys'. These locomotives did not have a power brake and every application and release of the engineís brake involved a lot of manual effort; there were many turns of the handbrake wheel and the steep gradient meant that the brakes had to be hard on at every stop.

The Magee's brewery siding was located on the High St. branch, and one of the tasks of the Crook St. shunter was to deliver water from Burton-on-Trent in special tank wagons that were tripped in via Atherton. The tanks were very rusty inside, and this, in combination with the high mineral content of the water, made it very unpalatable, but compensation was provided in the form of a free drink for the train crew at each delivery.

Train working at Crook St. itself involved an unusual procedure for the sorting of incoming trains. As the yard was a terminus the engine of an arriving train could not be used to break the train up into its destination sidings. The immediate approach to the yard was downhill, however, so arriving trains would stop prior to reaching the yard with the bulk of the train on the downhill section, where the ground staff would apply enough wagon brakes to hold the train while the engine uncoupled and ran forward into a spare road. By carefully releasing some brakes and applying others, the train could be cut up and each portion run into its correct road by

Plate 84. A general view southwards across the yard at Crook St. on 7th. December 1963. Judging from the number of wagons to be seen there was still considerable traffic at this time, but it was much reduced from that of former years. The yard shunter, Class 3F 0-6-0T No.47378, can just be seen behind the central row of vans. The cobbled paving between the rails in the foreground marks the site of the wagon turntables of former years, long removed at the time of this photograph.   Photo, Author.

gravity. As each portion was dispatched, the train was run forward as that part of the train that was on the slope could be used to draw the rear portion forward until it was also on a downhill gradient. The engine was rarely used to assist this process, as the shunters were very skilled and it became a point of honour to sort and stable a complete train in this way.

Shunting engines approaching Fletcher St. Jn (Bolton No. 2) box indicated their intended destination to the signalman by whistle code, 1 whistle and 3 crows, for example, signifying a wish to proceed from the old passenger line (alongside the passenger ramp) to the goods yard, thus crossing the running lines in the process. Access to the shunting neck of the yard itself was controlled by a mechanical gong operated by a lever near the shunter's cabin. The ramp to the passenger station could also be used for shunting purposes, up to 20 wagons being allowed onto the ramp in the down (to Gt. Moor St.) direction, with 25 allowed on the up line.

Plate 85. Crook St. yard from Fletcher St. bridge in May 1956. The ramp to the passenger station and Soho Foundry are dimly visible in the distance, and in the foreground are the water tank, the cattle dock, and staff amenities. The clerestory coach body in the immediate foreground is interesting but has so far defied identification.

Photo, G.J.Hardy.

Plate 86. Surrounded by coal, Class 8F 2-8-0 No.48745 shunts the yard at Adelaide St. in Bolton on 23rd. March 1965. Photography of trains at this location was always difficult. To avoid disruption of traffic on St. Helens Road the only working over this section of line was very early in the morning, in hours of darkness in winter, and it was therefore a dedicated photographer indeed who braved the chill of early morning to capture it on film.

Photo, H.J.Scowcroft.

LIFE AT PLODDER LANE

The gas lighting in the shed was very dim, but the only other means of illumination were duck lamps, which provided a very sooty and smelly yellow flame. These were used to ignite the gas lamps when the pilot lights failed (which they often did), and were also necessary for all examinations and repairs carried out underneath or inside the engines. Boilersmith Ernie Griggs made good use of duck lamps while caulking leaking stays inside the fireboxes of the coal tanks and 0-8-0 goods engines (the latter described as 'small ballrooms' in comparison with some fireboxes), and with both damper and firehole door open the draught was sufficient to clear the smell and fumes from the lamp

been used by Noah during construction of the ark. This venerable piece of machinery was powered by a shed labourer who, standing in a wheelbarrow so that he could use his body weight to help turn the operating wheel, would crank the handle for five or six minutes at a time in between rest breaks. With this minimalist equipment, aided by hammers, chisels, files and spanners, the fitters at Plodder Lane did miraculous work in keeping their ageing collection of locomotives on the road. L&NWR engines were particularly prone to leaking regulator valves, and as these were located inside the dome returning them to a steamtight condition involved removing the dome cover and dome. The latter often took several days if the securing nuts were seized onto the studs and had to be split using a hammer and chisel.

Plodder Lane Conservative Club was a favourite 'after-hours' meeting place for Plodder Lane staff, and during working hours the signal box at Hulton Sidings played

Plate 87. Class 5 4-6-0 No.45281, is approaching the steepest part of Chequerbent bank with an early morning train for Bolton on 22nd. July 1963. The platelayer's hut beyond the first bridge marks the approximate site of the former Chequerbent signal box. This once controlled access to a line diverging to the right behind the bridge that led to the Hulton Collieries Nos. 3 and 4 Bank Pits. Photo, J.Marshall.

through the boiler tubes and up the chimney.

The fitting shop, located along the back wall of the old shed, was quite small. It had a long bench running along one wall, with several vices and Plodder Lane's only machine tool, a large hand-powered bench drill, suspected by the staff of having

much the same role (but without alcohol!), providing opportunities for darts and card games between runs for crews on trip or banking duties. In the last years of the Little Hulton line, when it was being worked as a siding from Fletcher St., it was not unknown for engine and train to be left standing on the line at the site of Plodder Lane station while the crew took a 'personal needs break' in the Conservative Club nearby. On Sundays the station was closed, but the waiting room was used for various meetings of railway personnel. The most frequently held meeting was that of the first aid class, organised by Arthur Wells, who was one of the signalmen in Plodder Lane No. 2 box, and run by a local practitioner, Dr. Schofield. The mutual improvement classes for footplate staff were also held in the station waiting room on Sundays. These were organised by a local driver, Harold Ewell, who became such an expert on signalling matters that he was in demand as a speaker at other mutual improvement classes at such locations at Bury, Agecroft and Patricroft.

The following story may be just part of the Plodder Lane folklore, but as it came from two independent sources, one of whom knew the people involved, is worth retelling. Plodder Lane No. 2 box was in exposed area, and one very dark and windy morning the signalman had the windows closed and fire going well when two cleaners from the sheds used the instrument at the exit signal from the shed yard to send a bell code to the box 'engine for Bolton direction', then left the shed, walking between the rails, one carrying a white lamp pointing towards Bolton and the other, some distance behind his mate, with a red lamp pointing in the opposite direction. They stopped outside the box, shouted to the signalman (who did not appear) '4356, light engine for Springs Branch'. It was cold and pitch black, and the wind was howling, so hid any lack of noise from the 'engine'. The signalman set the route, sent the 'train entering section' message to Fletcher St., whereupon the cleaners quickly returned to the shed. The signalman in No. 2 box thought no more of the incident until the inevitable query came from Fletcher St. when the 'engine' failed to appear. The consequences were not trivial, as the line between Plodder Lane and Fletcher St. Jn. had to be closed and a train was being held up at Hulton Sidings. The shed foreman was called to organise a search party for the missing locomotive, and chose to send the two cleaners who had perpetrated the prank to walk the route and check for a disabled locomotive, which of course was never found!

Plate 88. In 1959, a L&NWR 0-8-0 heads away from Hulton Sidings with a short train for Bolton. The train has just passed the junction with the Booth's Steelworks siding, the course of which can be traced from the white gate by the guard's van across the photograph to disappear behind the slag heap on the right. The mining history of the area is evident from the slag heaps in the foreground. Recent reclamation schemes have obliterated any trace of the railway here and housing now exists on the former Booth's Steelworks site.

Photo, G.J. Hardy.

WAR-TIME WORK AT PLODDER LANE

During wartime the length of shifts was unpredictable, with twelve hours or more being common. On New Year's Eve 1943 passed cleaner Jim Jones was on the 09.00 cleaning shift, expecting to be finished at 17.00 in time for the season's festivities, but a spate of 'sickness' resulted in no fireman being available for the afternoon Atherton bank engine, due off shed at 16.00. Jim got the job and worked an L&NWR 0-8-0 light engine to Atherton, where there was 2-3 hours of shunting work to be done before trains for Bolton, which needed a push up the hill to Chequerbent, began to arrive at around 18.30. The relief crew for this turn booked on at 20.00, travelled to Bolton on the 20.20 from Plodder Lane, then took the 20.40 passenger to Atherton. The original crew were then scheduled to return by passenger train, finishing around 22.00. On this occasion, however, a derailment at Manchester led to late running of the train from Plodder Lane, and the relief crew missed the train to Atherton. Instead of requesting the banker to come to Bolton for the crew changeover, the relief driver and fireman decided without notifying anyone to catch the 20.55 to Manchester (passing through Plodder Lane again but in the opposite direction), alighted at Walkden Low Level, walked across to Walkden High Level on the L&Y line for a train to Atherton Central, then walked across Atherton to Bag Lane. In the meantime the crew of the bank engine at Bag Lane, with no knowledge of the whereabouts of their replacements, carried on pushing trains up the hill until just after midnight when the relief finally arrived. The last passenger train to Bolton had long since left, so the original crew travelled in the guards van of the last good train, leaving Atherton around 01.00, finally arriving back at Plodder Lane on the footplate of that train's engine after 02.00, for Jim Jones a shift that had lasted over 17 hours with no opportunity for a meals break after 16.00 the previous day.

Superimposed on the long and unpredictable shift working were the Plodder Lane Home Guard duties, a voluntary function involving one night per week on duty guarding the Plodder Lane goods yard and vicinity. The headquarters of the Plodder Lane Home Guard was the office in the goods shed, where a platoon of typically six men would meet at 20.00, but in practice 'guard duty' only began in earnest once the Conservative Club had closed, usually between 01.00 and 02.00, when the men would re-assemble in the goods shed office for a game of cards before going home at about 04.00.

At Plodder Lane, as elsewhere during the war, there was a severe staff shortage in all grades. This problem was exacerbated by a call from the management for footplate staff to transfer in order to fill much needed vacancies elsewhere. At Plodder Lane over half the firemen went elsewhere, four to Stafford and a larger number to Saltley in Birmingham. For those who stayed, this meant extra work and the shortage of firemen ensured that passed cleaners were fully employed on the footplate and very little if any cleaning was done. The shed itself was cleaned by 'Old Bill', long since past retirement age, whose routine consisted of starting to sweep at one side of the shed and a week later arriving at the other, with frequent stops in the mess-room along the way. 'Old Bill' was given two lady assistants during the war, but in reality there was little for them to do, and when two more were sent at a later date 'Old Bill' permanently took on the role of shed-sweeping foreman.

From 1942 Italian prisoners of war from the camp at Warth Mill at Radcliffe worked in both the goods depot and the engine sheds at Plodder Lane. They were brought daily by motor coach to the goods yard entrance, and about fifteen of the party walked unguarded across the running line to the shed, where they were employed on labouring duties but not allowed to assist directly with locomotive work (where ironically the need for manpower was greatest). As there was little non-locomotive work for such a large number of men, most of their time was spent sitting around talking until the motor coach came to pick them up in the afternoon.

During the war years and afterwards there were marked changes in the quality and quantity of coal provided at Plodder Lane. At the start of the war the main supplier was the Manchester Collieries, from Walkden Sidings or Sanderson's Siding. This coal was a mixture of two kinds, mostly average but containing a very small amount of high grade material that could be recognised by a distinctive 'herring bone' pattern in the grain. A good proportion of this high grade material was 'appropriated' for use in signal boxes (and even domestic grates!) The Manchester Collieries coal, while not equal in quality to best Yorkshire steam coal, was acceptable. It left a lot of ash and clinker, but the clinker was thick, heavy and rough and not difficult to lift from the firebars when cleaning the fire.

The increasing demands for good quality coal during wartime meant that Plodder Lane soon had to make do with material of lesser quality from Garswood Hall colliery, near Wigan. This produced a thin, sticky clinker, which ran between the firebars and which, after a few hours of firing, could block the grate completely. Worse still, when coal supplies were really low, the fireman had to use the thick, compacted material from the very rear of the tender, much of which had been there for years and had very little calorific value. Coke was also used at this period, but of course the fireboxes were not designed for it and its slow burning qualities made firing difficult.

Very occasionally a wagon of good Yorkshire coal would arrive at Plodder Lane, but word soon got around to signal boxes and stations in the area, all of whom requested a few cobs, so that workings from the shed soon took on the guise of a coal distribution exercise. At the other extreme was the introduction of coal briquettes from South Wales, originally made up in square blocks of 28 lbs. Their shape and size was dictated by the ease of packing into a ships hold, but meant that they required breaking up for locomotive use, a very dusty and dirty operation. They were slow burning and produced a lot of ash, but not much clinker. After protests from the unions they were provided in 7 lb. blocks, easier to manage but still disliked by the footplate crew.

A different kind of fuel was provided later in the war in the form of wooden blocks that had been removed from roadways. These had been used in place of stone cobbles to reduce the noise from horse-drawn vehicles. When such roads were resurfaced the blocks were taken up, and one method suggested for their disposal was to use them in locomotive fireboxes. The blocks were mainly oak, with some pine, and burned well but very rapidly, so much so that engines were coming back to the shed with empty tenders long before their shift was over. The Chequerbent bank engine managed only one trip up the bank with this fuel, and left the fields on both sides of the line ablaze! It soon became apparent that they were unsuitable for locomotive use, but as they had to be disposed of somehow the authorities kept sending them. The problem was eventually solved at Plodder Lane by the simple expedient of leaving wagons filled with the wooden blocks alongside the shed, the shed staff taking care of their disposal once it was discovered that the blocks were ideal for burning in a domestic grate! This method of disposal, devised by the shed clerk, solved the problem in a creative manner acceptable to all. Another shortage during the war was that of castor oil, used at Plodder lane for lubrication of the leather diaphragm in the vacuum-controlled regulators of the coal tanks. This was also considered by some staff members as a domestic 'prize' and 'leaked away' from the sheds according to need.

The bunker doors of the coal tanks were not well designed, and Plodder Lane men tended to fire the engines from the footplate, using coal that was brought forward from the bunker as required. 'Little and often' was the official term, but 'ample and continuous' was more accurate when working up the grade from Roe Green Jn. These engines were worked hard on the Manchester - Bolton trains. On receiving the 'right away' on the up grade from Walkden or Little Hulton the regulator handle would be opened wide, and on dark nights the progress of the trains could be seen from afar by the sparks thrown from the chimney of the coal tank as the engine accelerated, increasing to a veritable firework display as the train gathered speed. Many of the coal tanks were 'doctored' by the Plodder Lane fitters by having 'jimmies' fitted to the blast pipe to sharpen the blast and thereby increase the smokebox vacuum. The Plodder Lane version of the jimmy consisted of a bucket handle, cut and bent to fit inside the top of the blastpipe, but one driver, Rupert Foster, had a different solution. He would fill the base of the smokebox of his coal tank with old brick arch blocks, thus leaving the exhaust free but reducing the smokebox volume so that the air was drawn through the fire in sharper 'puffs'.

The coal tanks were by no means infallible, however, especially with the quality of coal sometimes provided in the 1940's. One Saturday in 1947 the evening train from Manchester Exchange to Bolton, a coal tank with five coaches, stalled at Roe Green just clear of the junction with the brakes leaked on, and sat for seven or eight minutes with the blower on before sufficient pressure was available to release the brakes and allow the train to continue. Fortunately it did not foul the catch points on the branch when it came to a stop, as the signalman had forgotten to release them before the train stopped (in the normal position there would have been a derailment had the train run back on restarting), and so had to carefully move them to the through position with the train sitting over the points.

During the early 1940's a coal tank had the interesting job of moving the stock of the 11.33 Manchester Exchange to Llandudno from Ordsall Lane sidings into Exchange station. The engine concerned, usually No.27590, would have arrived at Exchange with a train from Bolton at 08.53 and filled in on ECS work until returning to Bolton with the 12.07 departure. The job of moving the stock for the Llandudno departure was not a trivial one, as this train was composed of GWR carriages and usually handled by a GWR 4-6-0 locomotive, so would have the GWR braking system that required a greater vacuum to release the brakes than that needed for the LMS coaches for which the coal tank's vacuum ejector was designed. As a consequence, this duty could involve the coal tank moving a set of coaches whose brakes were not fully released, and was hard work for all involved.

Roe Green Jn. was protected by a fixed distant signal from the Bolton direction, but the corresponding home signal was almost always clear for trains from the Bolton direction by the time that they arrived at the junction. Working the 16.25 motor train from Bolton Gt. Moor St. to Monton Green one day in the early war years, the driver of a coal tank cheerfully ignored the fixed distant as usual, and consequently ran past the home signal at Roe Green, which, very unusually, was firmly at 'stop'. The brakes were slammed on hard as the train hurtled towards the junction points, which fortunately were set for the branch. The signalman at Roe Green just got the road for the train, and lowered the home signal to indicate the fact, as the train disappeared round the curve towards Sanderson's Siding. The next evening, the approach to Roe Green Jn. was made with absolute caution!

The replacement of the coal tanks with new locomotives was not viewed with uniform favour. Although the new LM&SR 2-6-2T's were more powerful and masters of their work, when they first arrived at Plodder Lane the men found them draughty, especially when working bunker first, which was likened by one former Plodder Lane man to 'riding a motorbike in just your underpants'. Plodder Lane crews solved this problem by tying pieces of wagon sheeting to the cab roof, but a permanent solution was eventually provided in the form of metal side pieces that were fitted above the rear hand rails.

During the summer months Plodder Lane men also had two seasonal workings, one involving a Manchester Exchange to Blackpool (via Tyldesley) train, worked by a Plodder Lane 4F 0-6-0, and the 08.10 from Exchange to Windermere, worked by a Plodder Lane crew who travelled 'on the cushions' to Patricroft, picked up an engine there, and worked the train to Preston, with a return working from Preston 'as required'.

Plate 89. The Atherton Pits Nos.1&2 of the Hulton Colliery Co. Ltd., were sunk adjacent to, and on the east side, of the Bolton & Leigh Railway in 1892 and 1897 respectively. In 1900 two more shafts, Nos.3&4, were sunk about 1/2 mile to the south-east and new connections made with the Bolton & Leigh mainline at Chequerbent from these new pits. In 1912 these four pits became known as the Bank Pits, to avoid confusion with collieries in Atherton, namely those of Fletcher Burrows & Co. No.4 pit came to be known as 'Pretoria' pit and this undated view of Pretoria shows a predominance of Hulton Colliery wagons. Pretoria Pit will forever be remembered for the worst mining accident that ever occurred in Lancashire when, on 21st December 1910, an underground explosion killed 344 men and boys. The slag heaps of Pretoria Pit are still visible today, to the north of the former Lancashire & Yorkshire's Pendleton-Crow Nest Jct. line, just west of Atherton station. Now overgrown with trees, they are a poignant reminder of the price of coal.

Photo, Triangle Publishing.

MOVING THE FREIGHT

The night fast goods train to Leeds was operated in the 1890's by a 'Jumbo' 2-4-0 allocated to Plodder Lane for the purpose and known locally as 'Johnny Dogan'. The origin of this name is a mystery as no L&NWR 2-4-0 had a name resembling it, nor was it derived from the name of the regular driver on this turn, one Livesey Hodgkiss, well known in the Plodder Lane area for he would blow the engine's whistle continuously from Plodder Lane station to Little Hulton Jn. as a goodnight message to his son, who would be going to bed around the time that the train passed through the station. Plodder Lane's largest goods engines from the turn of the century were the Webb compound 0-8-0's, known locally as 'Swamis'. Unlike the situation elsewhere, Plodder Lane crews generally got on quite well with these engines, which were considered 'all right' for the work in hand.

Freight engines in the down direction from Roe Green Jn. were worked just as hard, if not harder, than coal tanks on the passenger trains. Banking of the heavier freight trains was common, but occasionally a driver would attempt to lift a load in excess of the allowed maximum without assistance. Drivers with the L&NWR 0-8-0 engines, in particular, were often tempted to try their hand unassisted, providing audio and pyrotechnic displays as the engines roared through Walkden and Little Hulton on long cut-off and full regulator, but if the train stuck an engine had to be sent from Patricroft, with the inevitable delays that this entailed.

One unusual traffic handled at Bolton was wrought iron work from Walmsley's forge. Walmsley's was the last plant in the world to produce wrought iron by the traditional puddling process, and even when this process was discontinued they carried on producing wrought iron goods using old axles from wooden railways wagons as a source of material for re-rolling. During the wartime years Walmsley's was a centre for the re-processing of wrought iron railings from the scrap metal drive, but very little of this material could be re-used as it was often so fragile that it was destroyed by oxidation during the remelting process, and some of it was still on hand when the works closed.

The lighter side of freight train working is illustrated by a trip during late 1940's, when George Glover, a fireman at Plodder Lane, was waiting at Ordsall Lane with his Driver Arthur E. on the footplate of a Class 5 4-6-0 to work the 22.10 freight to Edge Hill, Liverpool. This train normally followed the 22.20 from Manchester, the Holyhead boat train as far as Earlestown, but on this occasion got clearance from the signalman to precede the passenger, provided the latter was not held up. The freight was moving nicely by the time it reached Cross Lane, near Eccles, and driver was leaning out of the window when, with a loud bang, a gauge glass broke and the footplate was filled with boiling water and steam. George found the shut-off handle, and was going to get a replacement glass from his bag when he noticed the driver mumbling and gesticulating. Finally, over the noise of the engine, the latter made it clear to George that when the gauge glass had exploded the bang had surprised him and caused him to spit out his false teeth, which were now somewhere on the lineside in the vicinity of Cross Lane station! Mindful of the Holyhead boat train only minutes behind them, the crew of the Liverpool freight had to keep moving, but on the return working it was dawn by the time they reached Cross Lane, and with distant signals against them George suggested to the driver that they slow down through the station, so that he could get off the footplate and look around for the missing items. Luckily, he found them on the ramp leading up to the platform, climbed back on the engine, and handed them back to the thankful owner who, after washing them with the slacker pipe from the tender, fitted them back in place and continued with the rest of the trip as if nothing unusual had happened.

PLODDER LANE 'CHARACTERS'

Like any other workplace, Plodder Lane had its fair share of characters. Some have already been mentioned, like Livesey Hodgkiss, driver of the Leeds goods in the 1890's, Bill Entwistle, who could be heard three fields away when whispering, 'Old Bill', the shed sweeper, Ernie Griggs the boilermaker. Another was Dick Croston, a fitter who took the new 60 ft. turntable under his wing and cleaned and greased the bearings so that it ran as smoothly as a sewing machine. Among the footplate grades there were pairs of men who, while excellent drivers or firemen when apart, just could not work together. Driver Billy Lever and passed fireman Jack Day were one such combination, and driver Charlie Beamish and Billy Bullock were another. At the time in question (1941) Charlie Beamish was in the top passenger link, so virtually had his own engine, shared with only one other driver on the opposite shift. Charlie was meticulous to a fault and it was his practice before leaving Manchester Exchange to chalk a number, usually in the 90's, on the back of the cab of his coal engine. This was the number of shovelsful of coal that he expected the fireman to use on the trip to Bolton, and he was rarely out by more than ten. Furthermore, he would instruct the fireman when to apply each shovelful, and even where in the firebox

it should be placed. While this was acceptable to some junior fireman, Billy Bullock was a senior man with over twenty years experience of goods work, and never happier than when his engine was blowing off steam with a full firebox. After some threats of physical violence, the two were discreetly split up! By way of contrast, Tommy Owen was an easy-going driver, happy to leave much of the responsibility of driving to his fireman while he did the latter's job.

Driver Harold Ewell was a master of his trade, as were Rupert Foster and Arnold Duxbury, who left Plodder Lane in the early 1930's for a move to Carnforth, but eventually returned to the L&YR sheds at Burnden. George Bibby was another dedicated driver, who had come to Plodder Lane from the L&YR sheds at Bury in the 1930's, and was delighted when the L&YR 2-4-2 tanks were allocated to Plodder Lane. The L&NWR men were just as delighted for George to take these engines out, as it meant that they did not have to use them! Passed cleaner Bill 'Kit' Carson was one of those unfortunate accident-prone individuals. When the wall on the west side of the shed was blown down one night foreman George Ball, on seeing the rubble when coming to work the following morning, said "I see that Carson is on nights again".

Plate 90. The entrance to the Magee, Marshall's siding, on the left, looking back down the High St. branch in the Bolton direction in September 1956. The footbridge in the distance was located close to Fletcher St. The catch points in the siding were very necessary at this location, as a runaway down the 1 in 37 incline could have had dire consequences.

Photo, G.J.Hardy.

ACCIDENTS

Fatal accidents on the Gt. Moor St. lines were fortunately rare, but on 31st. July 1935 a 17 yr. old junior porter at Gt. Moor St. station, Cyril Geeson, was taking a message from the station to Bolton No. 2 signal box, and to save time travelled from the station on the footplate of a light engine. It was a very murky day, even for that area, and on stepping down from the engine he did not see or hear the 09.55 motor train from Kenyon Jn. as it drifted along past the signal box with the engine at the rear, and was hit and killed instantly. His father, Cecil Geeson, was a signalman in No. 2 box but was not on duty at the time of the accident.

Signalling errors always carried the potential for disaster, and on two occasions in the 1940's Plodder Lane men were involved in such mishaps. In the late 1940's, a Plodder Lane crew was rostered to take the 17.05 local from Manchester Exchange to Leigh, shunt the empty stock into a siding at Kenyon Jn, and then proceed light engine to Atherton to work a freight train back to the Manchester Ship Canal Sidings. On one occasion George Glover was firing this turn on Jubilee 4-6-0 No.5563 *Australia*. It was dark by the time that the stock had been stabled with the brakes hard on against the buffer stops in a long siding running parallel to the Bolton line, and the engine, with the guard now on board, ran back to the signal box. The signals were cleared for Atherton, and the engine set off tender first, accelerating into the darkness. George had just put a round into the firebox and was pouring a drink from his brew can when there was an almighty crash as the locomotive hit something at speed, and the next moment he was picking himself up in a dazed state from the footplate, saw the driver behind the water scoop handle, his face covered in blood, and the guard unconscious in the tender, having been thrown through the coal doors. Help arrived, eventually in the form of an ambulance from Ashton-in-Makerfield, which took the unfortunate crew to Leigh infirmary. The driver's face was stitched, George was released, but the guard's injuries were

more serious. He never fully recovered, and was put on light ticket barrier duties at Manchester London Road, but regretfully died within months of the accident. The accident was caused by a signalling error. The signalman had been distracted by the presence of a trainee in the box, and although the signals for the line to Bolton were cleared correctly, the engine had been directed back into the sidings from which it has just emerged, and so rammed the empty stock that it had just deposited against the buffer stops.

Another accident involving the misreading of signals happened at Warrington in the first few months of the war. Driver Tommy Cash was working the Warrington turn, returning light engine from Arpley Sidings to Dallam shed, and passing Winwick Quay thought he was on the main line but was in fact running along the goods loop and reading the signals for the main line, which were cleared for a northbound express train. Running at some speed, the light engine crashed into a goods train, killing the guard and scattering wreckage onto the main line, where it was run into by the express train, fortunately without causing too much further damage. Several cattle wagons of the goods trains were damaged and most of the cattle killed; they were buried in an adjacent field.

Derailments during careless shunting were always to be guarded against, especially given the state of some of the track in the lesser-used sidings. A spectacular example of this occurred, however, not in a decrepit colliery siding but in the well maintained Highfield Sidings. A Plodder Lane passed fireman on his first driving job in the early 1940's had an L&Y A class 0-6-0 and was shunting the sharply curved sidings there, which required barrier wagons to be in place between the engine and the wagons to be moved, as the engine could not negotiate the sharp curves. The engine was on loan from Springs Branch, and of a type not very familiar to Plodder Lane men. In particular, the regular had to be pushed to open, whereas on L&NWR engines it was pulled, and the driver, forgetting both this and the need for barrier wagons, took the engine slowly into Highfield Sidings. On attempting to close the regulator, he instead opened it wide and left the rails, proceeding in a straight line across the cobbles to end up at the bottom of the yard, a long way from any rails!

The parting of a coupling on loose coupled and unbraked trains was a perennial threat, and could have dire consequences. On a gloomy, semi-foggy late afternoon in 1943, passed cleaner Jim Jones was working on the Atherton bank engine when a coal train from the south approached Atherton Bag Lane station. The station was located on a short section of relatively level track, but had a rising gradient on either side for up trains, and the driver had braked hard for signals, causing the wagons to buffer up, then while the train was still moving had opened the regulator wide as the signal was cleared. The resulting snatch caused a coupling to break, and the entire train of 30 loaded wagons started off back down the hill to Atherton Jn. The guard could not stop it and jumped clear, and the train ran away at high speed through Atherton Jn. until it reached a set of catch points, whereupon it was deposited in its entirety in heap down the embankment. The wreckage was close to a council housing estate, and when a train was sent several weeks later to clear up the mess, all they found were the axles, wheels and springs of the wagons. The coal and wooden parts had been put to good use elsewhere!

Early one evening in 1947 a goods train broke a coupling between Worsley and Monton Green, and although the front half could be safely drawn into the loop at the latter station, the rear half was stranded blocking the up main line. A coal tank had just left Roe Green Jn. running as light engine to Bolton, where it was to work a train to Kenyon Jn., but on an appeal from Monton Green was called back to propel the rear half of the goods train into the loop. The driver insisted on going onto Plodder Lane shed to take water, but was back at Roe Green by about 20.15, ran to Monton Green to move the stranded wagons, and then coupled up with the light

engine from the 17.45 ex. Bolton Gt. Moor St. to Manchester train, another coal tank. The two coal tanks were thus both delayed, and the drivers no doubt eager to finish their shifts, with the result that on the return to Plodder Lane they ran through Sanderson's Siding at close to the maximum line speed, both engines running chimney-first, briefly shut off steam to hurtle precariously through the points at Roe Green, and blasted their way, with couplings rods whirling, up the hill towards Little Hulton.

On lines with such steep gradients as those of the L&NWR in the Bolton area, the prevention of runaways down inclines required extra vigilance and strict adherence to the correct operating procedures. Runaways down Chequerbent incline were rare, but not unknown. One evening in the early 1940's the Atherton banking engine had dropped off the train at Hulton Sidings, and crossed to the down line to wait for a clear road back to Atherton. In the meantime, the signalman at Hulton Sidings accepted the evening freight from Bolton to Warrington, and while it made its way from Bolton, offered the freight to Atherton, having forgotten about the banker which was still standing on the down line waiting for the road. Atherton accepted the freight, all the signals were pulled off and the driver of the banker, thinking the road had been cleared for him, set off slowly tender first down the bank. Meanwhile, the Warrington goods passed Hulton Sidings with an apparent clear road ahead, and rammed the banker on the steepest part of the incline. Whether the crew of the banker jumped or were thrown off is not clear, but the engine, luckily not derailed by the collision, ran away through Atherton, Atherleigh, and Kirkhall Lane level crossing (which was fortunately open to the railway) and did not come to a halt until just beyond Westleigh station on the incline up to the Bridgwater Canal. No damage was done and the affair was kept quiet for a very long time afterwards!

Runaways down the inclines into Bolton had the potential to create havoc at the terminus, and this sort of catastrophe happened on several occasions.

The first recorded instance was in the late 1830's, when six wagons loaded with cotton ran away down the incline from Daubhill one evening. Fortunately, the points were set through to the Hulton coal depot, then located on the north side of Gt. Moor St., and the passenger station was spared. The second, more serious, incident involved the locomotive Redstart and train of goods and coal wagons, the resulting demolition of the passenger station in Bolton being instrumental in the decision to construct the new terminus at Gt. Moor St. in an elevated position. The next serious runaway took place on 16th. March 1918 when an 0-6-0 'Special Tank' with driver Arthur Barnett and a train of loaded coal wagons ran away down the grade into Bolton and crashed through the buffers at Crook St., subsequently demolishing the wall and ending up in the cellar of a house on the other side of the road. The engine crew jumped clear and no-one was injured, but property damage was substantial. In later years, Arthur Barnett's two sons, Arthur and Richard (Dick) both became drivers at Plodder Lane; his daughter Ivy was employed there during the war years as a tube cleaner, and two of Arthur Barnett senior's grandsons, another Arthur and Albert (Ivy's son) later became cleaners at the shed, so at least three generations of this typical railway family were employed there.

The last, and least well known accident of this type occurred in 1946, when in the early hours of the morning a Class 4F 0-6-0 with train consisting of sixteen loaded wagons and a brakevan, ran away down the bank from Daubhill. The driver was an undiagnosed diabetic, and had gone into a diabetic coma on the way down the bank. The fireman was a young passed cleaner on his first main line firing turn and was unaware of the danger and enjoying the speed as the train dashed into Crook St. yard and hit a row of brakevans on a storage road. On impact the engine was deflected sideways, demolishing wagons on the adjacent road, while the train went to the other side and demolished more wagons there. Notwithstanding having their brakes hard on the vans that were directly hit were pushed through the buffer stops and the wall into Crook St. The crew remained on the footplate on this occasion, and the driver, although severely shaken, was uninjured. He was transferred from footplate duties but the fireman, who lost two fingers in the accident, returned to footplate work and eventually retired as a main line driver around 1990.

An early example of an accident caused by wagons running out of control down a steep incline occurred at Little Hulton in May, 1875, shortly after the opening of the Little Hulton Mineral Branch but, although a L&NWR train was involved, the accident did not result in any damage to railway company property. At about 01.00 a L&NWR locomotive was working in the exchange sidings at the end of the Little Hulton Mineral Branch sidings at Wharton Hall Colliery when careless shunting resulted in nine wagons running out of control down a gradient of 1 in 20 towards Wharton Hall Colliery. The wagons apparently ran for 1100 yards, and at a speed estimated by the local newspaper reporter to be not less than 70 miles per hour crashed into a newly constructed engine shed housing the locomotive Graham. The shed was destroyed and the engine turned on its side, sustaining considerable damage. None of the runaway wagons survived, but fortunately the accident did not result in any personal injuries.

RELATIONS WITH THE BURNDEN SHEDS

For the major part of the 20th. century, Bolton had two locomotive sheds, for in addition to Plodder Lane there was the former L&YR establishment on Crescent Road, close to Burden Park (then home of the Bolton Wanderers football team). In pregrouping and LM&SR days there was considerable rivalry between the L&Y and L&NWR establishments, and even after the companies had ceased to exist many enginemen still thought of themselves as 'Lankie' or 'Wessie' men. Although it was not uncommon for Plodder Lane men to be out 'on loan' to Burnden, especially during the later years when work at the former establishment was beginning to diminish in volume, or transferred when promotion opportunities arose, this distinction remained, even after Plodder Lane had closed and some of the remaining staff had transferred to Burnden. It was also not unknown for Plodder Lane staff to be loaned out to Horwich Works to fire the works pilot engines. During the late 1940's the mutual improvement classes from Plodder Lane and Burnden sheds held joint trips to centres such as Derby works to improve working knowledge of locomotives and footplate techniques, but relations between the two sheds in Bolton were not always as harmonious.

Some Burden staff were inclined to look down on their 'lesser brethren' from Plodder Lane, and treated men on loan from the latter depot with a degree of disdain, amounting to hostility in some cases. Sometimes this was reflected in a patronising attitude towards the newcomer, with a barely hidden disbelief that anyone from Plodder Lane could know how to handle an engine, but sometimes the situation was worse. One of the more extreme examples concerns a Burden driver who consistently refused to speak to his fireman, on loan from Plodder Lane, even to the extent of not informing him where the train that they were manning was going or even what the departure time was. In the event, it was a local trip to Horwich and the fireman was able to thwart the driver by obtaining from the guard all the information that he needed in order to get the locomotive ready on time.

In December 1944 a landslip at Kearsley closed the line between there and Clifton Jn. for over a week, and during this time the extra burden of work that fell on Burnden sheds was alleviated somewhat by the loan of all the spare cleaners and passed firemen from Plodder Lane. Transfers from Plodder Lane to Burnden were possible during LM&SR days, and as they provided a faster route for promotion than staying at Plodder Lane several men took advantage of the opportunity, but rivalry between the two sheds remained healthy. One night, a gang of cleaners sneaked out from Plodder Lane sheds around 02.00 and walked the short distance down Bradford Road and into Crescent Road to the Burden sheds. There they picked an engine each, opened the dampers, put the blowers on and filled the fireboxes before leaving quietly again for Plodder Lane. As they made their way back up Bradford Road, they could hear the engines start to blow off one by one, and see large clouds of black smoke silhouetted against the moonlight. It would be several hours before the engines could be silenced, and complaints from the neighbourhood would surely follow!

Plate 91. The entrance to Sunnyside Mills at the bottom of Barrier St. The original Bolton & Leigh alignment ran over the top of this elliptically arched bridge but later terminated at the coal yard which abutted Adelaide St. *(See plate 70)*

Photo, J.Jones.

Plate 92. Passenger trains may have stopped running, but while freight service was operating, track maintenance was still needed. This view of work in progress on the down line at Rumworth & Daubhill illustrates several features, including the concrete sleepers (note the wooden sleepers of the up line), and the poor nature of the track ballast in use on many secondary lines at that time.

Photo, Tillotsons Ltd.

Plate 93. Demolition of the up (Manchester) side buildings at Plodder Lane is under way in this late 1955/56 photograph. The corner of No. 1 signal box is just visible behind the bridge. The coaching stock in the goods yard across the running lines is probably condemned and awaiting disposal. The workman on the right will have a long wait for the next passenger train- it was the LCGB special of 21st. September 1963 and only went as far as Little Hulton!

Photo, Tillotsons Ltd.

Chapter 6.

Decline and Closures

Plate 94 The frontage of Gt. Moor St. station on 7th. December 1963. The two large double doors gave access to the booking hall, and thence by stairway to the platforms. At the extreme right can be seen the gate which allowed access to the ramp leading to the end-loading dock. The end of the overall roof is just visible, giving a good impression of the height of the platforms above street level. Photo, Author.

CLOSURES BEGIN

The branch from Crook St. yard to Deansgate warehouse in Bolton closed in 1930, but it was not until the early 1950's that major changes took place on the former L&NWR lines in the Bolton area. Plodder Lane station was repainted in the then standard cream and maroon in July 1951 (but never received the new standard 'totem' station signs, a printed paper version for the noticeboards having to suffice) and the up line between Plodder Lane and Little Hulton Junction was relaid with new concrete sleepers in 1952, but the drastic decline in traffic following the wartime years resulted in redundancy of both men and machines, and Plodder Lane station and its engine shed were living on borrowed time.

Even as early as the 1930's it was clear that Bolton did not need two passenger routes to Manchester. Local tramway services were competitive for intermediate traffic on the Manchester and Leigh lines, and the former L&YR routes adequate for longer distances, for example to Liverpool. The passenger service between Bolton Gt. Moor St. and Tyldesley had already been withdrawn in 1942 as a wartime economy measure, never to be reinstated, and following the end of hostilities further cut backs were inevitable. The freight service was also in gradual decline, particularly on the goods side: in 1931, as part of a scheme to gain extra revenue from under-used resources, the LM&SR introduced a scheme to use land in 'depots that are lying idle' for the purpose of public car parking. The goods yards at Plodder Lane and Lever Street were included in this scheme, an area of 300 square yards being set aside at the latter, and an undisclosed amount of land at the former. The car parks were open during normal business hours, tickets being available from the goods agent's office at the rate of 1s.0d. for cars and 0s.6d. for motorcycles. There is no indication of the outcome of this initiative, but it is hard to imagine a significant demand for car parking space at Plodder Lane in 1931, unlike today when such a facility would prove a boon to car-congested Bolton: an idea far ahead of its time!

Plate 95. Class 8F 2-8-0's Nos.48770 and 48553 approach the signal box at Rumworth & Daubhill with a mineral train for Bolton on 9th. May 1964. The inclusion of a brake van at the head of the train may have been to facilitate shunting arrangements at Bolton, as part of the train would reverse there on its way to Little Hulton Jn.
Photo, I.G.Holt.

The stations at Rumworth & Daubhill and Chequerbent were closed to passengers on 3rd. March 1952, and only a short time later, on 27th. March 1954, the last regular passenger services ran between Manchester and Bolton Great Moor Street via Roe Green Junction, and between Great Moor Street and Kenyon Junction, resulting in closure to passengers of the Roe Green Junction - Bolton - Pennington lines. The Railway Executive anticipated the closure by the withdrawal, without notice, in 1952 of some of the trains between Monton Green and Bolton, but the loss of the passenger services was to be a protracted affair. In October 1952 the local councils received notice from the Railway Executive that passenger services were to be withdrawn from September of the following year: in November 1952 responses from the Worsley and Little Hulton Councils pointed out the inadequate nature of the replacement bus services, and noted that in view of housing developments along the Bolton-Roe Green route an improvement rather than loss of rail services was indicated. In April 1953, as a result of protests from the local councils and the Transport Users Consultative Committee, the Railway Executive granted a six month extension of passenger services, with slightly reduced fares but no increase in the number of trains. During this period the Farnworth Trades Council took up the fight. In response to their protests, they were informed in January 1954 that the Bolton - Manchester route was losing £16,000 per annum with revenues of only £1,700. In February, the Council organised their own survey of passenger use, and produced the following figures:

	Railway census	Council census
First train of the day, Walkden to Bolton	1	11
First train of the day, Bolton to Walkden	0	'quite a few'
First train of the day, Bolton - Manchester	5	105
Saturday night traffic, Bolton to Little Hulton	40	150

In addition, the Council pointed out that the line was under-utilised for excursion purposes. In recent months, only four excursion trains had been provided, one to Blackpool, two to Belle Vue (Manchester), and one football excursion for a Bolton vs. Manchester United match, all of which had been 'quite successful'. The Trades Council passed their case on to Farnworth MP E. Thornton, who is reported to have said the 'closure' is by no means a good idea, as roads, especially in South East Lancashire, are becoming too congested for safety'. One cannot help but wonder what his response would be to the same roads today! The protests, however, were in vain. The six month extension of services produced 'no appreciable response', and the closure took place as planned from March 29th., 1954.

The local councils were not finished with the matter, however, and the issue of reinstating passenger trains on the Bolton - Little Hulton - Manchester route was to resurface periodically for the next ten years. On April 6th. 1961, the Farnworth, Walkden and District Trades Council unanimously passed a resolution calling for the re-opening of the Bolton Gt. Moor St. to Manchester Exchange line for passenger trains, citing an increase in housing along the line, especially at Little Hulton and Plodder Lane, and the inadequacy of the bus services. This resolution was sent to the Ministry of Transport and to the local MP, the same E. Thornton who had fought to keep the line open, but the request fell on deaf ears and there was no response from British Railways. The question of reopening the Bolton connection surfaced again in

November 1963, this time in connection with TUCC hearings on the projected closure of the Manchester Exchange to Wigan route. The Eccles Trades Council pointed out that a much better alternative to closure would be the reopening of the line to Bolton, again citing the increase in housing developments around Little Hulton, and noting that this would be a better economic solution for the railways than the proposed closure. This proposal was supported by the Lancashire County Council, mainly on the grounds of reducing road congestion on the area, but again there were no positive developments and closure of the Wigan route to passengers took place. In 1965 the opportunity for reopening was irretrievably lost, as British Railways began discussions with local councils on the disposal of the land in question. As a consequence, in early 1966 the route from Roe Green to the Farnworth boundary was released for footpath and green spaces, while Farnworth Council took over the land within their jurisdiction for development. The site of Plodder Lane sheds was sold to the Land Development & Building Co. for re-development in April 1969. In Bolton, Hick, Hargreaves took over ownership of the land on which Crook St. yard was laid out in 1967, and Bolton Corporation began to buy the former L&NWR land in 1970, acquiring Lever St. yard in December of that year and the site of Gt. Moor St. station in March 1973. Land in the Fletcher St. area was acquired by Townson Developments Ltd. in August 1971.

Plate 96. Corrugated iron had a short life span in the atmosphere of Bolton in the 1950's and 1960's, so the roof covering the coal drops at Dawes St. in Bolton appears to be relatively new in this view taken on 7th. December 1963. The exterior wall of the passenger station can be seen on the left, and the town hall clock in the background. The houses on the right give an idea of the elevation of both Gt. Moor St. station and the coal drops at this location; coal lorries could be loaded directly from the wagons without the need for lifting the coal from ground level as was common elsewhere.
Photo, Author.

CLOSURES AT PLODDER LANE

Rail-borne freight traffic was also on the decline in the early 1950's, and with the ending of local passenger services on 27th. March 1954, Plodder Lane shed had no reason to remain open. The remaining shunting and freight duties could be handled from Patricroft or Wigan (Springs Branch), and Plodder Lane shed closed on 10th. October of that year, the first of the Manchester area sheds to do so following nationalisation of the railways. An immediate consequence was a wider variety of locomotives in the area; for the first time, the new BR Class 9F 2-10-0's appeared, the first reported being No.92103 in 1956, and both the WD - and LM&SR-designed 2-8-0 freight engines became more common.

The shed buildings at Plodder Lane were demolished soon after closure and the site was cleared by the District Engineer, but the tracks in the shed yard were left in place for some considerable time, not being removed until July 1964, at which time the rails were cut into short lengths in situ and the pieces removed by road via the goods yard. During the late 1950's the shed yard was used for storage of withdrawn wagons, many of which were broken up on site when, after a long period in store, their movement by rail was judged to be unsafe. As late as 1964 the locomotive inspection pits at Plodder Lane were littered with the remains of private owner's wagons registered by the L&NWR, L&YR, LM&SR, L&NER, Midland, and even the Caledonian and Great Western Railways. During the late 1950's the goods yard was used for storage of withdrawn coaches, examples being noted of coaching stock from the L&NWR, L&YR, Midland and North Staffordshire Railways, and until 1958 was also used for the storage of empty stock for excursion trains from Bolton Great Moor Street.

The Plodder Lane station buildings were demolished in 1954/55, soon after closure, but the goods yard remained officially open until 30th. January 1965 and the signal boxes and goods shed remained until that time. The section south of Little Hulton Junction, as far as Roe Green Junction, was closed for goods traffic on 24th. October 1960, and on 7th. May 1961, the signal boxes at Plodder Lane and Little Hulton Junction were reclassified as ground frames, the line from Lever Street box in Bolton to Little Hulton Junction being worked thereafter as a siding. The goods shed at Plodder Lane was out of use and boarded up in 1964 following several attempts at arson the last, on 5th. July, causing considerable damage to the office area. Plodder Lane No. 1 box had been boarded up around 1961, at which time many of the signal arms in the area were removed, and was demolished in 1967. No.2 signal box, servicing the goods yard, continued in use as a ground frame despite have been damaged by fire on 6th. July 1964, although in view of the fire-damaged interior of the goods shed at that time it is unlikely that the yard was used very frequently. The signal box at Little Hulton Junction was damaged by fire in 1963, but remarkably survived, albeit derelict, until April 1969, when it was the subject of another arson attack and finally destroyed.

FREIGHT WORKINGS IN DECLINE, 1954-1965

The pattern of freight services did not change substantially for some time after the closure of Plodder Lane shed in 1954, as duties and locomotives were transferred to Patricroft. In some cases, the same locomotives continued to do the same jobs they had performed prior to the closure, a notable example being Class 3F 0-6-0T No.47401, a long time Plodder Lane engine, that frequently came back to shunt Crook St. yard after being transferred to Patricroft on the closure of its former home. Times were changing outside the world of the railway, however, and the consequences of such change would inevitably make their mark on the railway. The mining industry was in decline, and much of the traffic at this time, particularly on the Little Hulton line,

consisted of loaded or empty mineral workings. A reduction in need was reflected by a reduction in capacity. The signal box at Walkden Sidings had not been manned since the mid-1950's, a signalman travelling with the train to open the box as required, and Walkden Sidings had been little used for some time when the line south of Little Hulton Junction was closed to all traffic in 1960. By 1962 the remaining freight trains on this section, summarised in Table 18, were few and far between. The Scowcroft coal business at Highfield Sidings continued to generate some traffic, as did the exchange with the colliery lines at Little Hulton Junction, but there was little additional demand for freight service south of Bolton in the Little Hulton direction.

Table 18. Extract from the Working Timetable, Freight Services between Bolton and Little Hulton, September 1962., Up Line

		9T68	0T71	9T71	9T60
			SX	SX	SX
Bolton	Dep.	07.25	11.58		14.15
Fletcher St. Jn.	Pass	07.28			
Lever St.	Arr.	07.32	12.03		14.20
	Dep.	07.52		12.13	14.30
Plodder Lane	Arr.	07.57			
	Dep.	08.20			
Highfield Sidings	Arr.			12.21	14.40
	Dep.			12.36	15.08
Little Hulton Jn.	Arr.	08.26		12.41	15.13
Notes		A	B	C	

A: stops at Highfield Sidings as required
B: engine + brake
C: stops at Plodder Lane as required

Down Line

	9T68	9T71	9T60
		SX	SX
Little Hulton Jn. Dep.	08.45	12.56	16.15
Fletcher St. Pass	08.56	13.10	16.25
Bolton Arr.	09.00	13.15	16.30

Note that at this time the "T" designation in the train reporting number indicated a local trip working. Table 18 shows a clear pattern of out-and-back workings from Bolton, servicing Lever St., Plodder Lane and Highfield Sidings as required in the up direction, collecting traffic at Little Hulton, and then returning non-stop to Bolton. This was the pattern that would be maintained until closure of the section in 1964/65.

The end of the 1950's saw freight traffic on the Atherton line from Bolton in a healthier state than its counterpart on the Little Hulton section, but still precarious. The section between Atherton Jn. and Pennington South Jn. was closed to all traffic on 17th. June 1963, but was still included in the summer 1963 working timetable, which is summarised in Tables 19 and 20. With the undoubted proviso that this timetable more

accurately portrays the workings of the previous year, it shows that through trains to Liverpool were still in operation, and a daily goods train to and from Warrington ran, but the latter required light engine movements from Warrington (Dallam sheds) in both directions. The principal change in comparison with earlier years, however, is the extent to which operations at Hulton Sidings had declined. By the 1960's the local pits were either closed or being phased out of operation, and this decline in production is reflected in the train services. Also notable is the number of light engine movements to and from Patricroft sheds. Closure of the direct link between Roe Green Junction and Little Hulton Junction may have saved some track maintenance, but the resulting accumulated light engine mileage and time allowances were considerable.

Table 19. Extract from the Freight Working Timetables, June 17th. to September 8th. 1963, Down Line

		MSX	MO		MX	SO	SX	SX	SX	SX	SX
Bolton Arr.		06.05		09.20	09.30	11.05	11.58	14.10	16.38	17.00	18.10	18.25
Fletcher St. Jn.		06.09		09.22	09.34	11.08	12.01	14.15	16.40	17.04	18.13	18.27
Rumworth & Arr.		06.16										
Daubhill Dep.		07.30										
Hulton Sidings Arr.		07.40			09.41			14.25		17.13	18.23	
Dep.		09.30										
Chequerbent												
Atherton Bag Arr.		09.50			10.00	11.28	12.19			17.25	18.35	
Lane Dep.			08.15	09.34			12.21			17.32		
Atherton Jn.			08.18			11.43	12.23	14.43	16.57	17.37		18.43
Fletcher's Siding												
Westleigh Arr.								14.54				
Dep.								15.10				
Pennington S. Jn.			08.31	09.49				15.17				
Kenyon Jn. Arr.			08.36	09.55				15.24				
Notes			A	B	C	D	E	F	G	H		I

148

Passing times are shown in italics

A: to Edge Hill (Liverpool).

B: LE to Warrington after working the 06.42 from Warrington.

C: from Little Hulton Jn. dep. 08.45.

D: Empties To Bamfurlong. Stops at Hulton Sidings and Chequerbent as required.

E: Two light engines to Patricroft; one from Bolton, couples to one from Atherton.

F: 12.56 SX from Little Hulton Jn. Stops at Atherton and Fletcher's Siding as required.

G: LE to Patricroft after working the 16.15 from Little Hulton Jn.

H: to Warrington via Tyldesley

I: L.E to Patricroft

Table 20. Extract from the Freight Working Timetables, June 17th. to September 8th. 1963, Up Line

				MO	MX	SX	SX	MX	SX	SX	SX	SX
Kenyon Jn.				07.50				12.30			15.34	
Pennington S. Jn.				08.00				12.38			15.38	
Westleigh												
Fletcher's Siding												
Atherton Jn.	05.30	05.41	05.57	06.31	08.10		11.34	12.00	12.50			15.47	
Atherton Bag Lane Arr.		05.46	06.00	06.33	08.13		11.36	12.05	12.55				
Atherton Bag Lane Dep.		06.15	06.02		08.33	10.15	11.38			13.25	13.55		17.15
Chequerbent						10.25							
Hulton Sidings Arr.		06.33	06.11		08.48	10.36				13.42	14.10		
Hulton Sidings Dep.					10.46								
Rumworth & Daubhill													
Fletcher St. Jn.	05.50	06.46	06.19		09.10	10.50	11.53			13.54	14.22	16.00	17.37
Bolton Arr.	05.52	06.50	06.21		09.05	10.53	11.55			13.58	14.25	16.03	17.40
Notes	A	B	C	D	E	F	G	H	I		J	K	L

Passing times are shown in italics

A: LE from Patricroft dep. 05.00

B: from Ordsall Lane dep. 05.00

C: two light engines from Patricroft dep. 05.30; one uncouples at Atherton.

D: LE from Springs Branch dep. 06.15

E: from Warrington dep. 06.42

F: shunts at Chequerbent, 10.25 to 10.33

G: LE from Patricroft dep. 11.05

H: from Burton dep. 06.40

I: mineral from Edge Hill dep. 11.20. Suspended

J: runs as required

K: LE from Dallam sheds to work the 17.00 to Warrington

L: stops at Hulton Sidings as required

The timetables summarised in Tables 19 and 20 confirm the survival at this late date of two long-established railway traditions at Bolton connected with the remnants of the Bolton and Leigh line. Table 19 shows that the 06.05 Bolton to Atherton stopped to shunt at Rumworth & Daubhill, running down to the Adelaide St. coal yard and thus regularly disrupting the early morning traffic as it shunted across the ungated crossing on St. Helens Road. Table 20 shows the arrival at Atherton at 12.05 of the 06.40 from Burton. This train carried the water in tank cars that was later tripped to the Magee, Marshall's Siding in Bolton. Local water in Bolton was too soft for brewing traditional beers, hence water was regularly imported from Burton-on-Trent for this purpose.

Plate 97. (right) In the early 1960's, a Class 8F 2-8-0 leaving Bolton is seen passing No. 2 signal box. On the right is the siding connection to the Atlas Forge, and in the foreground are the remains of one of their shunting engines, the 0-4-0ST *Phoenix*. This venerable locomotive, of unknown origin, had been at Atlas Forge since at least the 1870's. Its remains occupied the siding shown here for ten years before they were finally disposed of in 1970.

Photo, Bolton Museums and Art Gallery.

Plate 98. (left) A BR Class 5, 4-6-0 is seen shunting the sidings of Hick, Hargreaves Soho Foundry in the mid 1960's. The locomotive is working along the original course of the Bolton and Leigh passenger line at Bolton; the later ramp to the new Gt. Moor St. station can be seen on its left. The empty sidings on the far right, known as the Mission Sidings, were used for the traffic handled at the Bridgeman St. warehouse, behind the photographer.

Photo, Bolton Museums and Art Gallery.

FINAL CLOSURE OF THE L&NWR SYSTEM IN BOLTON

By June the 1964 much of the Lever Street Goods yard area was rented out for non-railway use, although the signal box was retained to control access to the Plodder Lane and Little Hulton Junction ground frames. Traffic beyond Lever Street in the Manchester direction was limited to the occasional trip to Plodder Lane, Highfield Sidings, and the Little Hulton mineral branch, but lingered on for some considerable time as long term contracts, particularly with Scowcroft's at Highfield Sidings and Benniss' Engineering work on the Little Hulton Mineral Line, were in place which obliged British Railways to continue a service which was, by that time, uneconomical for the railway. Complete closure from Highfield Sidings to Little Hulton Junction, including the Little Hulton mineral branch, took place on 11th. May 1964, although it was some time since trains had regularly ventured beyond Highfield Sidings for traffic purposes, running to Little Hulton Junction in the later months only for operating convenience to allow the locomotive to run round the train . In spite of having closed four years earlier, however, the down line south of Little Hulton Junction was still in place and was not lifted until February/March 1965, when it was used by demolition trains to lift the remaining rails.

BR were finally able to buy out the Scowcroft's contract, and the section from Fletcher St. Junction to Highfield Sidings officially closed for all traffic on 1st. July 1965. It was not until 1966, however, that the tracks were removed in the Plodder Lane and Lever Street areas, and through the tunnel back to Fletcher Street, and the last remnants of the Little Hulton Extension Railway were gone. By a strange quirk of bureaucracy brought about by their dependant ground frame status, the signal boxes at Plodder Lane and Little Hulton Junction remained 'open' long after their operation had ceased, not being officially closed until the box at Lever St. was closed on 13th. June 1966, by which time track

lifting on the line was complete. The tunnel from Lever Street to Fletcher Street was shored up internally by the use of concrete pillars, and the ends sealed off.

In Bolton itself, closure was a protracted affair thanks to agreements with private siding users, mainly the National Coal Board as successors of leases granted to the Hulton Colliery Co. High Street yard had closed for coal traffic on 1st. March 1947, but was used thereafter for rail traffic from Watson's Steelworks, and the tracks remained in place until closure of the Magee, Marshall's siding, which took place officially on 13th. October 1965, although trains had not used the siding since 1964. Crook Street yard was officially closed to British Railways traffic from 26th. April 1965 but continued in use to serve private sidings for the NCB until October 1967. Track lifting by a train in charge of 0-6-0 tank locomotive No.47378 took place in Great Moor Street station in April 1964, six years after the last excursion train had used the station, although the coal drops to the east of station remained in use well into 1965, closing officially on 14th. August of that year. Bolton No. 1 signal box was retained as a ground frame until 1st. October 1967, when all traffic into Crook Street yard ceased, although No. 2 box had been closed earlier, on 3rd. July 1967, following fire damage. Great Moor Street station buildings were finally demolished in October 1966, over 8 years after passengers from the last train had used them, and the bridge over Crook Street was removed in December of that year.

For the last two years of its life the track between Crook St. yard and Rumworth & Daubhill was worked as a single line, following a landslip between the tunnel mouth at Bolton and the site of Rumworth & Daubhill station that blocked the up line. Adelaide Street coal yard remained officially open until 2nd. September 1965, although trains had not ventured north of Daubhill coal yard for several months prior to that date, and the signal box at Rumworth & Daubhill had been closed on 24th. April 1965 as a result of fire damage.

From the summer of 1965 until final closure in 1967, Bolton was served by a single daily train that worked in from Patricroft in the morning, shunted the Dawes St. coal drops and Crook St. yard, collected any traffic on offer (usually coal empties), and then left Bolton around 11.30 for the return trip, pausing to shunt the coal sidings at Rumworth & Daubhill before running non-stop to Atherton. Traffic was then collected at Atherton before the train returned to non-stop Patricroft. This working was often rostered for one of Patricroft sheds Br. Class 5, 4-6-0's, resulting in the sight of one of these large engines shunting a few wagons at Dawes St. in Bolton, a job which for many years saw nothing larger than an 0-6-0 tank engine. Daubhill coal yard remained open until 30th. June 1967, but the entire section from Hulton Sidings to Bolton (Crook Street) closed

only a short time later, on 16th. October 1967. Trains from the Atherton direction continued to serve the Hilton Gravel Co. siding at Hulton Sidings until 6th. January 1969, requiring that a banking engine from Patricroft shed run light on a daily basis to be stabled at Atherton Bag Lane. The last rail-borne traffic in the area consisted of motorway construction materials, moved from quarries in Derbyshire in bulk train loads to Atherton and then split up into smaller loads to be tripped up the Chequerbent incline to the Hilton Gravel Co.'s siding. On 6th. January 1969, however, all lines north from Howe Bridge and Atherton Junctions were closed. It was perhaps a fitting end that part of one of the earliest railways in the country was instrumental in constructing its replacement mode of transport, and in the process survived to see the end of mainline steam traction in August 1968, a fine record of achievement for a notable section of railway and the men who promoted, built and operated it.

Plate 99. A Class 8F pauses by Lever St. signal box on its way to Bolton in the 1960's. The entrance to Lever St. sidings is on the right, but appears to have seen little traffic for some time. The home signal on the up line is a survivor of a L&NWR example, many of which were still to be found in the Bolton area into the 1960's.
Photo, Bolton Museums and Art Gallery.

Plate 100. The west side of Bolton Gt. Moor St. station on 7th. December 1963, looking towards Crook St. The angled wall identifies the course of the ramp leading from Gt. Moor St. to the end-loading dock of the station, the entrance to which was by means of the double gateway in the left foreground. The outer wall of the station was an impressive brick construction. Unfortunately there was no corresponding wall on the eastern side, as this was occupied by the Dawes St. coal drops. Photo, Author.

Plate 101. An overall view of Bolton Gt. Moor St. station from No. 1 signal box on 7th. December 1963. The end-loading dock is on the left, and the Dawes St. coal drops, with wagons in situ, are visible on the right. Although the signal arms have been removed, the posts from the starter signals of the 1940's re-signalling are visible on the platforms. The centre island platform was the same length as the longer outer platform when built, but was extended at an unknown date between 1882 and 1891.

Photo, Author.

153

Plate 102. The Manchester platforms, 3 and 4, at Bolton Gt. Moor St. station on 7th. December 1963. Platform 4 is on the right, and the air-raid shelter built during the second world war is clearly visible.
Photo, Author.

Plate 103. Bolton No.1 signal box on 7th. December 1963. An early example of a standard L&NWR signal box design, Bolton No.1 was built in 1874, and controlled access to Gt. Moor St. station for many years. However, by 1963 it had been relegated to a ground frame, released by Bolton No.2 (Fletcher St.) box, but continued to control access to the Dawes St. coal drops until it was closed on 1st. Oct. 1967.
Photo, Author.

Plate 104. A view from the Plodder Lane bridge, looking towards Bolton, on 19th. September 1965. Rusted rails are mute reminders of the fact that the line had been closed for several months, since 1st. July 1965. The track in the former engine shed area, behind the fence on the left, had been removed the previous year but the running lines and the goods yard were to remain intact for almost another year began track lifting and building demolition began.
Photo, Harry Jack.

Plate 105. A view of the area formerly occupied by the original four-road shed building at Plodder Lane, taken on 21st. July 1964, with the site of the later six-road shed on the right. The boundary wall on the south side of the shed area is clearly shown. The goods shed, located across the running lines, is also visible.
Photo, Author.

Plate 106. The site of the later 60 ft. turntable at Plodder Lane, on 21st. July 1964. The 'cut-and-carry' method used for the removal of the rails from the shed area is evident in this view. Plodder Lane is visible in the background with, to the right of the gap in the row of houses, the Plodder Lane Methodist Church with its wooden extension, the latter used in later years as a pre-primary school for local children.

Photo, Author.

Plate 107. The Plodder Lane bridge, looking southwards along the running lines, on 21st. July 1964. No. 1 signal box stands in the shadow of the bridge, and the remains of the up platform of the station can be seen just beyond the bridge. The tall post on the left once carried a L&NWR lower quadrant signal, but the signal is now gone. On the right at this location another signal once controlled the line to Bolton, but this was removed some time prior to 1929. Photo, Author.

Plate 108. The area of Walkden Sidings, looking towards Bolton in September 1964 four years after closure, is overgrown but still intact. The former through lines are in the foreground, with the colliery connection trailing in from the left and the exchange sidings across from the signal box. Photo, G.Hayes.

Plate 109. Track lifting in progress at Walkden Sidings on 13th. March 1965. This view, looking southwards towards Manchester, shows the former connection from the colliery lines on the right, now terminating at buffer stops. The signal box is derelict and leaning precariously, but a tall L&NWR lattice signal post still stands by the up line.

Photo, Author.

Plate 110. The Deansgate warehouse of the L&NWR in Bolton during demolition in early July 1963. Although closed for railway use as long ago as 1930, the warehouse continued in use, latterly for the storage of building materials by Mason's, a firm of contractors. The key feature in this view is the wagon turntable, buried under the asphalt floor covering but emerging intact from years of disuse. Unfortunately, it was not saved. Note also the massive steel girder framework construction of the building.

Photo, C.B.Golding.

Plate 111. Plodder Lane No. 2 signal box, on 21st. July 1964. In spite of having its windows boarded up and the interior damaged by fire the box was still officially open, although relegated to ground frame status. The running lines are in the foreground. The larger of the two huts is shown on track plans dating from 1891, and is thought to have been built at the time of the six-road extension to the engine shed.

Photo, Author.

Plate 112. The site of Plodder Lane station, looking northwards towards Bolton, on 21st. July 1964. The lower-level section of the right hand (up) platform identifies the site of the former station buildings. The goods shed in Plodder Lane yard is visible through the bridge that carried Plodder Lane over the railway, and the wooden section on the right hand side of the otherwise brick-built bridge parapet locates the site of the former booking office and station access from Plodder Lane.

Photo, Author.

Plate 113, (right.) Track lifting underway at Plodder Lane in April 1966. Class 8F 2-8-0 No.48553 is on the down line; the up line and entrance roads to the south end of the goods yard have already been removed, although No. 1 signal box is still standing.

Photo, H.J.Scowcroft.

Plate 114, (left.) The track had already been removed from the former shed area at Plodder Lane when the through lines were lifted in April 1966 by a train in charge of Class 8F 2-8-0 No.48553. The coaling plant and water tower are still intact, but now devoid of rails.

Photo, H.J.Scowcroft.

159

BIBILOGRAPHY

Given the relative obscurity of Plodder Lane, a remarkable number of published sources contain information on the subject. The following have been consulted in the preparation of this book. Where the information appearing herein differs from previously published details, it has been rechecked with primary sources and the present version is believed to be correct, but any remaining errors are of my own making.

✓ Bardsley, J.R.; The Railways of Bolton. Published by the Author, Bolton, 1st. Edn. 1960, 2nd. Edn. 1981.

Baxter, Bertram; British Locomotive Catalogue 1825-1923. Vols. 2A and 2B. London and North Western Railway. Moorland Publishing Co., Ashbourne, 1979.

Bolger, Paul; BR Steam Motive Power Depots. Ian Allan, London, 1981.

✓ Booth, T.; Baseboard Basics and Making Tracks. Silver Link Publishers, Peterborough, 1993.

✓ Booth, T.; Creating the Landscape. Silver Link Publishers, Peterborough, 1994.

Bradshaw's Railway Guide. Collection of issues held at the Manchester Central Library, 1875-1955.

Gray, Joseph W.; Railway Rates and Charges. Corporation of Bolton, Bolton, 1887.

Golding, Cyril; A Curious Place. British Railways Illustrated, May 1995.

Hawkins, Chris and Reeve, George; LMS Engine Sheds. Vol. 1. The London & North Western Railway, pp.179-180. Wild Swan Publications, 1981.

Hayes, Bob and Geoff; Plodder Lane 'Claughtons'. Push and Pull (Keighley & Worth Valley Rly Preservation Society), Spring 1995 (with follow up correspondence in the Summer and Autumn 1995 issues).

Hooper, J.; London Midland Sheds in Camera. Oxford Publishing Co., Poole, 1983.

Jack, Harry; Plodder Lane. L&NWR Society Journal, December 1994.

✓ Marshall, John; Forgotten Railways, North West England, pp. 8-16. David & Charles, Newton Abbot, 1981.

Signalling Record Society; British Railways Layout Plans of the 1950's, Vol 9. Signalling Record Society, Coventry, 1996.

✓ Simpson, Bill; Railways in and around Bolton. Foxline Publishing, Stockport, undated.

✓ Sweeney, Dennis; A Lancashire Triangle. Part 1. Triangle Publishing, Leigh, 1996.

✓ Sweeney, Dennis; A Lancashire Triangle. Part 2. Triangle Publishing, Leigh, 1997.

Townley, C.H.A., Appleton, C.A., Smith, F.D., Peden, J.A.; The Industrial Railways of Bolton, Bury and the Manchester Coalfield. Part 1. Bolton and Bury, pp. 19, 20, 31-33, 42-44, 53-58, 65-71, 74-101. Runpast Publishing, Cheltenham, 1994.

Townley, C.H.A., Appleton, C.A., Smith, F.D., Peden, J.A.; The Industrial Railways of Bolton, Bury and the Manchester Coalfield. Part 2, pp. 313-323, 337-415. The Manchester Coalfield. Runpast Publishing, Cheltenham, 1995.